£5.95

The World of Rugby League

The World of Rugby League

DAVID HODGKINSON and *PAUL HARRISON*

with a contribution by Mick Stephenson

London
GEORGE ALLEN & UNWIN
Boston   Sydney

First published in 1981

GEORGE ALLEN & UNWIN
40 Museum Street, London WC1A 1LU

© David Hodgkinson and Paul Harrison

British Library Cataloguing in Publication Data

Hodgkinson, David
  The World of Rugby League.
  1. Rugby football – History
  I. Title   II. Harrison, Paul
  796.33′3′0904   GV944.85

ISBN 0–04–796059–0

Set in 10 on 12 point Times
by Nene Phototypesetters Ltd, Northampton
and printed in Hong Kong
by Colorcraft Ltd

Contents

Photographs

9

We would like to thank the *Rugby Leaguer* – and, in particular, chief photographer Gerald Webster – for help in compiling the photographs for this book. Thanks also to the *Sun* and *Daily Mirror* for the use of their pictures. We also pay tribute to the work of Irvin Saxton and the Record Keepers' Club whose statistics proved invaluable in writing this book.

The World of Rugby League

CHAPTER ONE

Dedicated to the game

The sun-kissed beaches of Australia's southern tropics; the splendour of cosmopolitan Sydney with its majestic Harbour Bridge and graceful Opera House; the awesome beauty of New Zealand's North and South Islands; the fascination of southern France's wine-tasting paradise and the rugged charm of England's industrial north all have one thing in common – they play host to the greatest game in the world, Rugby League.

It is the game which was banned in France during the war years by the German-backed Vichy Government of Henri Philippe Petain and only kept alive by the village teams playing in areas of slack Nazi rule. It is the game outlawed by the Rugby Union throughout the world and the game which also turns Australian sportsmen into dollar-mad super stars.

Yet, in England, the Rugby League player is just the guy next door. He is the part-time professional who combines the long hours of a regular occupation with the rigours of twice-a-week training and a strength-sapping season that can see him play as many as fifty matches in eight months. The money he makes from the game can turn an average living into a good one, but it certainly won't give him untold wealth and, make no mistake about it, a Rugby League player earns every penny he gets.

It is not so many years ago that Great Britain players, who had just beaten France 10–9 in Toulouse, were told they would have to pay for their jerseys. After the game all fifteen jerseys went missing – they were either exchanged for French jerseys or not returned – and the League sent out a letter to each player warning that they might have to forfeit part of their £30 pay. The League estimated they had lost £100, £80 for the jerseys and £20 for eight pairs of football socks! Not exactly the best way to treat players in the world's toughest sport. For Rugby League is American grid-iron football without the padding. It breeds discipline, dedication, team spirit and, above all else, courage.

The game itself is synonymous with courage. In the legendary 'Rorke's Drift' tour of 1914 Great Britain won the Third Ashes-deciding Test with only ten men, and forty-four years later the Great Britain skipper, Alan Prescott, played all but four minutes of a Test match against Australia with a broken arm. His courage helped Britain to level the series and go on to retain the Ashes. Stories of courage abound in a game which brings out the true character of players – and referees.

English referees have earned the respect and admiration of the whole sporting world by their fair and firm handling of this rugged and physical game. Their word is final and such is the discipline of players that punishment is virtually always accepted with little more than a shrug of the shoulders. Certain soccer players would do well to take note! Yet even the referees show their own special brand of courage, especially in France where they have had to face the wrath and anger of ultra-partisan, bottle-throwing fans.

1. Huddersfield referee Billy Thompson leading England and France out for the 1980 European Champion-ship decider in Narbonne. Ninety minutes later he was locked in his dressing room, hidden from an angry crowd.

Top referee Billy Thompson reckons he shattered the 100 metre world sprint record as he raced for the safety of the dressing room after one heated and emotional European Championship match in Toulouse in 1970. That incident followed another heated game in Perpignan when Oldham referee Dickie Thomas was stoned by an angry French crowd and, although he had to spend the night in hospital, things would have been much worse had the Welsh players not moved in to help him off the field.

Incredibly, referees can even laugh and joke after such frightening scenes. A couple of years ago referee Thompson took charge of a European Championship deciding match between France and England in Narbonne. Late in the game he disallowed a try by the French and was greeted by a barrage of beer cans. Thompson shrugged off the trouble saying, 'They might have thrown full ones.'

At the time referees received only £15 plus expenses for taking charge of a senior game – hardly a King's ransom. Often the game's top referees will take charge of amateur and schoolboy games for nothing. Thompson has refereed matches all over the world in front of crowds approaching 100,000. Such big matches have often been

14

2. While waiting for the angry crowd to disperse at Narbonne the English team played charades.

followed, the next day, by schoolboy games watched by a handful of spectators, the groundsman and a couple of mongrel dogs. That is dedication.

Then there is the kind of dedication shown by Yorkshire referee Andrew Wardrop who lives in London but can only claim expenses from Doncaster which, for administrative purposes, is his base. He had to run the line at an 'A' team match at Tatters Field and journeyed up from London for the game, an expensive round trip of some 350 miles. His expenses for the game were just eight pence, the cost of a return bus ride from Doncaster town centre to Tatters Field.

Players, as well as referees, often have to put up with a great deal – especially from vociferous, excitable fans, but little could compare with what the Great Britain amateur team had to face in Papua New Guinea. It was on a hot, clammy and showery May night in Papua New Guinea that Britain's South Pacific tourists staged their own dramatic and alarming version of 'Napoleon's retreat'.

The BARLA Tourists were playing Northern Zone at Lae before 5,500 excitable fans crammed into the Rugby League Oval. Six minutes remained, the Papuans were winning 4–2, a couple of Britons had been sent off and the match was burning on a short fuse. Suddenly, as home referee Matt Tigaili signalled another Papuan penalty – he gave three to the British, thirty-four to Northern Zone – the balloon went up. Hundreds of angry, screaming locals, many wielding big sticks, stampeded across the pitch and attacked the British players. 'I thought we would end up in the pot,' said Ronnie Carter. Loose forward Paul Dowling was in the thick of the action. 'It frightened the life out of me,' he recalls. 'I thought about doing my bit and meeting the menace head-on, but there were thousands of them – a real "Charge of the Lae Brigade". Discretion's the better part of valour. I turned and ran.'

Paul and skipper Bob Colgrave had already attempted to rescue centre Dennis Oaten, who had been trampled beneath the furious onslaught and eventually, bruised, bloodied, but unbowed, the Britons barricaded themselves in the comparative safety of the dressing rooms. Outside the locals chanted and threw bricks. Inside, true grit and stiff upper lips to the fore, the bold Britons sang 'Rule Britannia' in loud, defiant tones.

England's professionals faced a similar fusilade of fury in a European Championship match against France at Narbonne in 1980. Huddersfield referee Billy Thompson had disallowed what would have been a winning French try for a forward pass. The

15

3. The BARLA tourists line-up before leaving on their history-making tour of Papua New Guinea, Australia and New Zealand.

notoriously passionate and partisan fans questioned the decision on the grounds that the referee is never right. They reacted angrily after the match and both Thompson and the English team were locked in the safety of the changing room until tempers cooled. The English barely raised an eyebrow at the wrathful commotion – they played charades.

Rugby League football in Australia has grown into a near full-time professional sport with some players earning more than £25,000 a year. Currently, the super-fit 'Kangaroos' rule the world and their players and coaches will go to great lengths to ensure they stay on top, both at international and club level. Some of their training techniques have to be seen to be believed, and coaches go to extremes to get their players motivated. One coach actually got his players to hit each other before playing; another got his team to kneel and pray.

Sadly, the lure of the dollar in Australia has led to some players taking drugs but, yes, the rewards are that high. Passion for the game of Rugby League can be displayed in a variety of ways. A young Australian player was banned for life when his passion got the better of him. After a particularly vociferous disagreement with a referee, the player stormed over to the trainer's bench, grabbed the bucket of water and poured it over the surprised official, 'I just can't seem to get through to you!' he said.

The introduction of sponsorship has brought a far more professional approach to Rugby League in recent years – from both players and officials. During the early seventies in Britain there were cries that the game was dying and that before the turn of the decade several professional clubs would have dropped out of the League. Attendances were falling fast, turnstiles were beginning to rust up and clubs were having to dig deep into their fast diminishing coffers to survive.

Then, suddenly, big businesses became interested in ploughing money into the game. Now every competition in Rugby League has financial backing and a great deal of the credit must go to League secretary David Oxley and Public Relations Officer David Howes. They had the foresight to see that for the game to progress it needed money from sources other than the turnstiles. The League's Council also deserves praise for the way it backed up Oxley and Howes. For the players the advent of sponsorship and flourishing club lotteries and pools meant greater rewards. Now, players can pick up more than £1,000 a man for triumph in the Cup Final at Wembley.

16

Rugby League, in Britain especially, now stands on the threshold of a glorious future. It has always been the aim of the English League to see its sport develop and expand further than the four Northern Counties of Lancashire, Yorkshire, Cumbria and Cheshire. The League would like to see Rugby League played nationwide before the game celebrates its centenary in 1995. The 1980 decision by the London soccer club, Fulham, to buy themselves a professional team and enter the Second Division brought the League's dreams a giant-sized step nearer reality.

More soccer clubs, faced by a decline in attendances and much needed revenue, started to sit up and take notice of the Fulham venture. It was the breakthrough that Rugby League needed; the chance to show people south of Doncaster what they had been missing for so many years. The bandwagon was rolling – and who can now say when it will stop?

CHAPTER TWO

Northern Union to Rugby League

William Webb Ellis. Now there was a rebel if ever there was one. In 1823, playing soccer at Rugby School, the bounder picked up the ball and ran clutching it to his chest. Thus were laid the foundations of rugby football.

A tablet of stone at Rugby serves as an eternal reminder of that momentous occasion. It reads: 'This stone commemorates the exploit of W. W. Ellis, who with a fine disregard for the rules of football as played in his time first took the ball in his arms and ran with it, thus originating the distinctive features of the Rugby game. A.D. 1823.'

It's a curious fact that rugby was born of a rebellious act and it was another act of rebellion, the Northern Union breakaway of 1895, which led to the birth of Rugby League.

A unique piece of sculpture salutes that piece of history; it is fixed to the wall in the reception at the George Hotel in Huddersfield, where the insurgents met for their mutinous meeting on 29 August of that year. Twenty-one clubs were represented including sixteen who are still members of the Rugby League – Batley, Bradford, Dewsbury, Halifax, Huddersfield, Hull, Hunslet, Leeds, Leigh, Oldham, Rochdale Hornets, St Helens, Wakefield Trinity, Warrington, Widnes and Wigan. The other five clubs have since slipped into oblivion – Brighouse Rangers, Broughton Rangers, Liversedge, Manningham and Tyldesley.

Mr H. H. Waller of Brighouse took charge and there was a near unanimous verdict – resignation from the Rugby Union. Only Dewsbury voted against as the rebels decided to form the Northern Rugby Union. This, then, was the breakaway – an irrevocable step into sporting conflict; a move to end two bitter years of infighting; a move which would be remembered as the first skirmish in a cold war which has split the handling code for close on a century.

The great divide developed because of what is termed 'broken time payments'. Rugby Union, born in a public school, had evolved as a gentleman's game, run by a hierarchy in the 'old school tie' tradition. The Union was officially formed in 1871, the year before the death of William Webb Ellis, and grew rapidly into a national pastime. But in the industrial north of England a social problem was unfolding.

There the game was enthusiastically played by the working class who began to claim expenses in lieu of lost time at work. Such was the agitation that on 20 September 1893 the Union called an emergency meeting at the Westminster Palace Hotel in London. J. A. Millar and M. N. Newsome, both representing Yorkshire clubs, proposed that, 'Players be allowed compensation for bona-fide loss of time.' An amendment was immediately proposed decrying the compensation call as 'contrary to the spirit of Rugby Union'. Of the 418 people at the meeting 136 voted in favour of broken time payments,

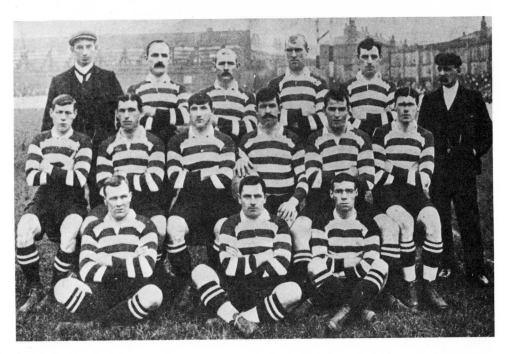

4. Broughton Rangers, the only team to win the Challenge Cup (then Northern Union Trophy) who are not now in existence.

but the resolution was lost. Several clubs instantly resigned. The Union, fearing professionalism, tightened its own rules to exclude any form of payment within the game. Professionalism had suddenly become a dirty word.

This, then, was the backcloth to the 1895 breakaway. Northern officials, recalling the 136 votes in their favour at the London meeting, sensed a major revolution against the governing body. Stockport and Runcorn joined the Northern Union in its first days and on 3 September the clubs met again, this time at the Spread Eagle Hotel in Manchester, to sort out their own rules and regulations. One of their first decisions was to declare themselves vigorously against professionalism and they set a ceiling of six shillings (30p) on broken time payment. Players, they declared, must find their own employment, the Northern Union game would be strictly amateur.

On 7 September the Northern Union kicked off with ten matches:

Batley	v	Hull
Bradford	v	Wakefield
Broughton Rangers	v	Wigan
Leigh	v	Leeds
Liversedge	v	Halifax
Runcorn	v	Widnes
St Helens	v	Rochdale
Stockport	v	Brighouse
Tyldesley	v	Manningham
Warrington	v	Hunslet

19

5. Dally Messenger, who guested with the All Golds in 1907.

6. Lance Todd, the wily half-back who played for Wigan.

7. Albert Rosenfeld, who scored a remarkable eighty tries in one season.

8. Jimmy Lomas, who moved from Bramley to Salford for a record £100 in 1901.

At the end of that first season the go-it-alone Northern Union (the Rugby Union had barred their member clubs from playing the rebels) had grown dramatically and at the annual meeting in August 1896 Mr H. H. Waller, the sport's first chairman, reported

9. Leigh's John Woods, rated the world's first £100,000 player.

fifty-nine member clubs. First honours went to Runcorn, who took the Lancashire Senior Competition title, and Bradford club Manningham were the Yorkshire champions.

In their second season the Northern Union introduced a new competition, something which was to become one of the phenomena of the British sporting calendar. It was the Northern Union Challenge Cup, now played at Wembley before a capacity 95,000 crowd and watched by millions throughout the world through the medium of television.

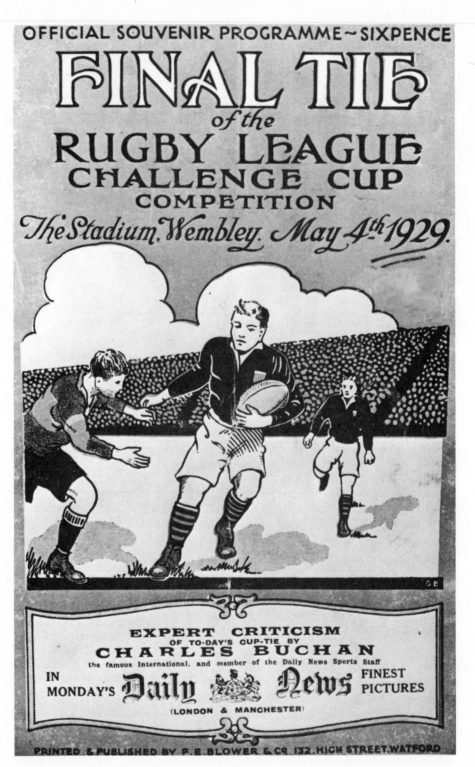

10. Front cover of the first Wembley RL Final programme.

11. Dewsbury's 1929 Wembley line-up.

12. Wigan's 1929 Wembley line-up.

Even that first competition captured the imagination of fans in the dying years of the nineteenth century. The first final, between Batley and St Helens, was staged at Headingley, Leeds, on 1 May 1897 before 13,000 fans who paid a total of £620. Batley, known as the Gallant Youths, won 10–3; meanwhile, Broughton had taken the Lancashire Senior Competition title and Brighouse were the Yorkshire champions.

The mood of the Northern Union was rapidly changing. The rugby babe had grown up and was ready to cut itself, finally and irreversibly, free of its parental ties with Rugby Union. It was a time of sweeping changes in the Northern Union rules. The scoring system was altered – three points for a try, two for a goal (drop, penalty or conversion) – lineouts were abolished and there was an experiment of kick-ins from touch. There was

13. Action from the 1930 St Helens–Widnes Cup Final at Wembley.

also a hint of the coming of professionalism in a tightening of discipline, particularly with regard to kick-off times. The spectator was becoming a vital cog in the Northern Union machine.

It was the Cup Final, the second NU Cup Final in 1898, which pointed the way towards professionalism. Headingley was again the venue. Batley reached their second successive final and their opponents were Bradford who were beaten 7–0. But the most important figure of the afternoon was the 27,941 crowd, who paid the princely sum of £1,506 for the privilege of watching the match.

Three months later, in July 1898, at the annual meeting in Huddersfield, the Northern Union took up the professional game. It was decided that all players must be registered and that they must have alternative employment. It was felt that it was dishonourable for a man to earn his living solely from playing rugby, and the Union was near-Victorian in the restrictions it applied to its employment regulation. Serving behind the bar at a public house was not termed suitable employment and a player from Radcliffe was banned when it was discovered that this was how he earned his daily bread. A Batley player failed to find work of any description and was banned from playing for two years.

The Northern Union continued to flourish with membership close on a hundred and new clubs joined in from the new territory of Cumberland. Players were well paid, too, with top stars earning up to £5 a match – far more than soccer stars of the day. Soccer, today's national game, paled in comparison in those far-off days. Headingley, that mecca of sport in Yorkshire, used to boast a soccer section. But that shut down towards the close of the century due to lack of support. In the early years of this century it was the round-ball game which captured the crowds and rugby clubs began to flounder in a pool of parochialism.

To 'Go National' was a Northern Union dream – and so it would remain until Fulham

24

14. Wigan, including the legendary Jim Sullivan, report for training on Southport sands before a Cup Final appearance in the thirties.

15. Hull, runners-up to Leeds in the Challenge Cup Final of 1923.

16. Leeds – 1905 vintage.

17. One of the first Cumberland County Championship teams.

in 1980. Instead, in 1901, a new league was launched involving clubs from Lancashire and Yorkshire who combined in two divisions of eighteen for an experimental period of three years. In 1905 the Big League was introduced with a full-scale championship and end-of-season play-offs. A year later came the most revolutionary change in the history of the game.

In a bid to make the game more exciting for the fans there had been experiments with a twelve-a-side game. This idea was, along with a St Helens proposal for fourteen-a-side, rejected – the magic figure was to be thirteen, a proposal made by Warrington and seconded by Leigh.

18. Rugby League secretary-general David Oxley's predecessors – by about seventy years. Northern Union officials from the early days.

The sport began to touch the rugby hearts of the Welsh who had, hitherto, treated the new game with scorn. Indeed, Welsh officials, inflamed by 'poaching' of their top stars by the Northern Union, had at times turned angry words into violent action when scouts from 'Up North' were discovered in their domain. Many a scout was bodily removed from a none-too-friendly clubhouse; some, it is rumoured, were pelted with snowballs or tomatoes and rotten eggs, all depending on the season of the year and/or the availability of garden and farm produce. One scout from Wigan was said to have been ducked in the sea and rolled in the sand, but six Welsh clubs took the plunge and joined the Northern Union. They were Merthyr Tydfil followed by Ebbw Vale, Barry, Mid-Rhondda, Aberdare and Treherbert. But they failed, mainly because of the high cost of travelling and when Ebbw Vale resigned in 1912 the Welsh adventure was ended.

Another adventure had, however, already begun with the advent of the sport in the Antipodes. Five years earlier, in 1907, the famous All Golds of New Zealand had made their historic first tour of Britain, calling off in Australia to play three Tests where they were guaranteed £500. The game had become an international sport.

The Kiwis included among their illustrious number two players destined to make an indelible mark in the new code – H. H. 'Dally' Messenger, an Aussie who was guesting with the party, and Lance Todd, a wily half-back, later signed by Wigan. His name is now remembered through the Lance Todd Trophy, awarded annually by the Red Devils Association to the man of the match in the Wembley Cup Final and regarded as the most prestigious award in the game.

The tourists, fired by their enthusiasm for the new game, found the thirteen-a-side rules difficult to master and, after losing several club matches, lost the First Test at

19. Prop forward Dave Chisnall celebrates following Warrington's 1974 Wembley triumph against Feather-stone. Dave is a non-smoker!

Headingley in January 1908. But they stormed to a Second Test triumph at Stamford Bridge, Chelsea, and won the decider at Cheltenham to win the first series. It was a victory to sweeten the expected news from the other side of the world – the New Zealand Rugby Union had banned all the tourists.

Australia made the breakaway in 1908, several months after a three match series in Sydney against the Kiwis. It was the New South Wales RU who made the bold step –

28

20. The men who led the Rugby League to Wembley – secretary John Wilson and chairman Mr F. Kennedy.

again following discontent at the 'broken time' ruling – and prepared for a tour to Britain later that year.

The Australians arrived in Britain in September, their squad captained by Dennis Lutge and including Dally Messenger and the legendary Albert Rosenfeld, a winger, who later joined Huddersfield and became a 'great' in a great team. In 1913–14 he scored a staggering eighty tries – a record likely to stand for ever.

The Northern Union, ever hopeful of going National, planned their three Tests at venues in London, the North-East and the Midlands. The team drew 22–22 at Park Royal in London before a dismal crowd of 2,200, but groans turned to delight at St James's Park, the home of Newcastle United, when 22,000 watched the Northern Union triumph 15–5. The final Test at Villa Park, Birmingham, the soccer stadium of Aston Villa, attracted 9,000 fans. Australia lost 6–5 and thereby lost the series 2–0.

Several representative matches were played against the Aussies on that tour – and each was played right in the heart of soccer territory, including games at Everton on Merseyside and Celtic Park, Glasgow. The Northern Union hoped this would kindle enthusiasm for the game outside the Lancashire–Yorkshire borders. No one took the bait until Coventry three years later – and that club lasted only two seasons.

Meanwhile, transfer fees were beginning to make headline news. Bramley's Jimmy Lomas, later to become Britain's first Tour captain, put his name into the record books when, in 1901, he moved to Salford for a record fee of £100. Twelve years later, with the dark clouds of war hovering over Europe, Billy Batten's move from Hunslet to Hull for £600 astounded the sporting world. Then, as now, Hull were the big spenders.

It was not until 1929 that rugby scored its first £1,000 transfer – that of S. Brogden from Bradford to Huddersfield. Mick Sullivan's transfer from Huddersfield to Wigan

21. Dewsbury's Second World War emergency line-up with (pictured centre) secretary-manager Eddie Waring. They won the Challenge Cup in 1943, beating Leeds.

nearly touched the £10,000 barrier, and in 1980 Hull made a shock £100,000 bid for John Woods of Leigh. The offer was refused. While transfer figures crept steadily upward, so discipline in the rugby game was tightened. Never were the rules more stringently applied than in 1911 at Watersheddings where Oldham were playing Barrow.

After only ten minutes of the match the referee sent off all thirteen Barrow players 'for wearing dangerous equipment'. Apparently, the team sported fashionable cricket belts, complete with metal buckles, to hold up their pants. They were later allowed to resume the match; it is rumoured that the players used odd bits of string and coloured elastic with dexterity to prevent further embarrassment.

Meanwhile, Huddersfield were fast developing into a great side, winning the championship three times in four years between 1911 and 1915 with Rosenfeld never knocked from his perch as the game's top try scorer. In 1911–12 he scored a record seventy-eight touchdowns including eight against Wakefield on Boxing Day. The next season he notched fifty-six, then came his historic eighty and finally another fifty-six in 1914–15.

The terrors of the First World War intervened. Several fine players lost their lives during the fighting and, after the hostilities ended in 1918, Runcorn, one of the founder members of the Northern Union, became peacetime casualties. They were not among the clubs who returned to rugby for the 1919–20 season and they were never again to play the thirteen-a-side code as professionals.

The period between the wars was to become a time of great change. In 1922 the code committed its parochial background to the history books and turned to the future with a new name: Rugby League. Since the game was no longer one played within the Northern boundaries of England, but also in Australia and New Zealand, the title Northern Union was no longer applicable.

That same year saw the birth of Wigan Highfield, later to play as London Highfield in the famous White City Stadium – an ill-fated attempt to take Rugby League to the capital. Highfield eventually returned 'home' to become known as Liverpool Stanley,

30

then Liverpool City and then Huyton – a luckless club through more than half a century.

Perhaps the most important milestone in the game's history was reached in 1928 when the authorities elected to take the Challenge Cup Final to Wembley, which five years earlier, in 1923, had staged the FA Cup Final for the first time. It was a momentous decision for the Rugby League and in 1929 Wigan and Dewsbury contested the first Wembley Rugby League Final, Wigan winning 13–2 through the talents of Johnny Ring and Jim Sullivan. Since then, except for 1932, Wembley has been the setting for Rugby League's showpiece final.

The 1932 interruption came about because of a British tour to Australia which necessitated an April Cup Final. Wembley authorities decided it was too close to the soccer final and Rugby League returned North – to Wigan, where Leeds and Swinton fought a close fight before Leeds won 11–8. Sad Swinton, they have never since appeared in the Cup Final and so have never played at Wembley!

In 1934 France entered the Rugby League arena with the legendary Jean Galia leading the way for 'La Ligue Française de Rugby à Treize'.

Twelve months later Acton and Willesden and Streatham and Mitcham became the newest London clubs on the Rugby League circuit. The Streatham side swooped into the market to snap up five Kiwi stars including George Nepia, an outstanding Maori full-back. Acton and Willesden dropped from the scene rather rapidly, to be replaced surprisingly by Newcastle in the North-East. But by 1938 both Newcastle and the enterprising Streatham and Mitcham had fallen by the wayside and a year later the Rugby League lost St Helens Recreation, a club deeply in debt.

The 1939–40 season began with the arrival of the Kiwi tourists, but they played just two matches – at Dewsbury and St Helens – before returning home. War had been declared. Play during the war years was severely restricted. However, in January 1943 Headingley staged one of the most fascinating rugby matches of all time – a League versus Union game watched by some 8,000 spectators. The game, between members of the war services, was played under Union rules – the League side winning 18–11 with a late scoring flourish.

The Second World War was followed by a rugby boom with big crowds and great matches. The boom was to last well into the fifties and was highlighted in May 1954 with the Challenge Cup Final. Halifax and Warrington had drawn a drab match at Wembley and the replay was scheduled for Odsal Stadium in Bradford. The official crowd of 102,569 staggered the Odsal officials who were totally unprepared for such a sporting invasion. Thousands were locked out as Warrington won the match thanks to the dazzling skills of Gerry Helme who won the Lance Todd Trophy.

Rugby League in Britain would never see such crowds again but ahead were seasons of change and excitement. The World Cup was introduced in that same year of 1954. Later, substitutes became an accepted part of the game. The four-tackle rule was introduced, later to be extended to six tackles. Two divisions came into operation in the early sixties but lasted just two seasons. In the seventies they were re-introduced, this time as a permanent fixture.

Sunday Rugby League was given a trial in December 1967 with Leigh as pioneers. Their match with Dewsbury was to have been the first match on the Sabbath, but they were upstaged by the Bradford–York and Featherstone–Salford fixtures which were played the same day. The Sabbath was to become the sport's saviour.

Television, with the inimitable Eddie Waring at the microphone, gave the sport to the nation, and sponsorship took the game by storm in the seventies with the John Player tobacco company setting up their own competition and giving Rugby League a massive shot in the arm.

The arrival of Fulham in 1980, a Rugby League team based on a soccer club, has set the pattern for the eighties. Soccer has again taken to the oval ball. William Webb Ellis lives on!

CHAPTER THREE

Rugby League 'Down Under'

Australian Rugby League rules supreme! There is no arguing with that after their resounding Test series triumph of 1979, when they won all three matches against the Best of Britain. Before that whitewash, which included a shattering 35–0 First Test annihilation at Lang Park, Brisbane, the Kangaroos had carried off the World Cup in 1977 and had retained the Ashes for the second successive time. While Britain always has and always will produce the skilled player, he is hardly a match for the ruthless run-through-a-brick-wall tactics of his Aussie counterpart.

It is hardly surprising that the Kangaroos are all-conquering – they even go to the lengths of appointing a hypnotherapist in their quest for glory. Roy Masters, coach of top Sydney club Western Suburbs, caused a major uproar when a TV documentary revealed how he created 'hate' motivation by urging his players to hit each other before going out to play a match. One shot in the film clearly showed a player attacking his team mate's throat, while another rained blows at a colleague's head.

Another Kangaroo coach, Warren Ryan, lifted his team to near boiling point by playing the theme from the blood-and-thunder boxing film, 'Rocky', as his players pummelled large sandbags on their way through the tunnel before a match. Paul Braughton, while coaching another Sydney side, Newtown, took a totally opposite approach in his build-up to Premiership games. He ordered his top stars to kneel and pray before a match, chanting 'Win, win, win . . .'.

But back to that hypnotherapist. During former Great Britain star Mick Stephenson's days at Sydney's Penrith club a dubious gentleman by the name of 'Cunningham' introduced the 'swinging pendulum'. His opening session had the Penrith players rolling around in fits of laughter – not the effect Mr Cunningham had expected. He persuaded the players to hold hands in a circle with their eyes closed as he chanted how strong and fit the team would be and how fast and confident they would be when the first whistle sounded. He then had all the players lying on the floor and, with the aid of gentle music and soft words, encouraged them to relax. It worked too well – Aborigine half-back Terry Wickey fell asleep and began snoring. Needless to say, Cunningham was rather rapidly given the boot. Yet he turned up at Canterbury the following year!

It's all a far cry from the early days of Rugby League in Australia. The formation of the game came largely as a result of an injury to Rugby Union international Alec Burdon. Burdon broke his shoulder during an Australian State game and received no compensation for time lost from work, nor for medical attention; this lack of feeling aroused a lot of well-known sportsmen, not least one of Australia's greatest cricketers, Victor Trumper.

22. British tourists from 1928. The four St Helens players are Alf Ellaby, L. Fairclough, A. Frodsham and Ben Halfpenny.

This furore came about in 1907 – twelve years after the Northern Union breakaway in England. At the time a New Zealander, A. H. Baskerville, was preparing to lead a team of Kiwi Rugby Union players across the world to England to play the Northern Union clubs. This tour created a great deal of interest in Sydney and Victor Trumper suggested that the New Zealanders play three matches in Australia on their way to England. The offer was accepted and the three matches were played under Rugby Union rules at the Sydney Agricultural Ground. A profit of £180 was made and the professional game was on its way in Australia. It was decided that the money should be used for publicity purposes, but the real breakaway came in 1908 when the New South Wales Rugby Union decided to form its own set of rules and send a team to Britain, the proceeds of which would be used to launch the NSW Rugby League.

The first season saw the formation of seven clubs, Balmain, Cumberland, Eastern Suburbs, Glebe, Newtown, North Sydney and South Sydney. Newcastle formed a side to complete tne line-up for the first Rugby League competition in Sydney. At the close of the 1908 season arrangements were made for an Aussie side to tour England; included in that side was Dally Messenger who was one of the big successes of the New Zealand tour the previous year.

The tour was a failure financially, but the Northern Union had underwritten the losses. A good number of Aussie players joined English clubs where they became great favourites, including the legendary Albert Rosenfeld, who joined Huddersfield.

In 1910 the Northern Union made its first trip overseas to Australia – a fact which

34

A. JUSTICE   C. FIFIELD   F. LAWS   L. SELLARS   A. RIDLEY   P. MADSEN   W. BROGAN   G. BISHOP   . A. HENDERSON
D. V. O'DEMPSEY   G. TREWEEKE   L. V. ARMBRUSTER   A. S. HENNESSEY (Coach-Trainer)   J. KINGSTON   H. STEINOHRT   W. SHANKLAND   W. SPENCER
J. UPTON   P. MAHER (Vice-Captain)   J. LORNE DARGAN (Joint Manager)   HARRY SUNDERLAND (Joint Manager)   T. GORMAN (Captain)   F. McMILLAN   E. ROOT
A. E. G. EDWARDS   E. WEISSEL   J. BUSCH   J. HOLMES   H. KADWELL
PHOTO FIELDING, LEEDS

23. The 1929 Australian tourists with joint managers Lorne Dargan and the famous Harry Sunderland.

fired the imagination of cloth-capped, working-class rugby players, who saw the dream of a round-the-world trip coming within their grasp. So many players were nominated by their clubs as potential internationals that two trial matches were held before the twenty-six strong party of players was named.

The First Test on Australian soil was played at Sydney on 18 June 1910 before a crowd of 42,000. The Northern Union battled to a tremendous 27–20 triumph. The second clash between the two sides was at Brisbane and again, watched by 18,000, the tourists clinched a terrific 22–17 victory. As the Test series was then won, it was decided that the third international match be played against a combined Australian and New Zealand team in Sydney, a match which finished all-square at 13–13. The Australians took scant revenge when they won an extra match 32–15 and the tourists went on to New Zealand, where they thrashed the home international side 52–20 before a crowd of 20,000 at Wellington.

These tours are a vital part of the Rugby League calendar. Australia and Britain are regarded as the top Rugby League nations in the world, and the mythical 'Ashes', which are at stake whenever the teams meet in a Test series, are the most prized possession on the international scene.

24. Stevo! The Great Britain and Dewsbury hooker Mick Stephenson who, in 1973, was transferred to Australian club Penrith for a then-world record £20,000. Mick is pictured at his proudest moment with the League Championship Trophy, won by Dewsbury six months before he moved to Australia.

The game in Australia has really prospered over the years to become the major winter sport in New South Wales and the Sunshine State of Queensland. Not that the game is solely restricted to these two areas. It is played all over the vast country from Perth in Western Australia to Adelaide in the South to Darwin in the Northern Territories as well as in Melbourne and Victoria. The game was introduced to Western Australia in 1948 and has now become the second sport in the state behind Australian Rules. In the early fifties South Australia took up the game and after several lean years there was a mini revival in 1976 with several new teams being formed.

Rugby League has a real fight on its hands against the Rules game in both South Australia and Victoria, but remains the number one sport in the Northern Territories with clubs in both Darwin and Alice Springs. Although the game is widespread throughout the huge state of Queensland, it is in New South Wales and its capital, Sydney, where sporting superstars are made.

The game around Sydney has grown into a near full-time professional sport with

25. Castleford player-coach Mal Reilly scores a memorable try against St Helens following his return from playing in the Sydney Big League.

26. Former Rugby Union hooker John Gray clearing the British line before his move to play in the Sydney Big League.

27. The triumphant Ashes-winning Australian tourists of 1978 led by Warrington-born Bobby Fulton.

players getting more than £25,000 a season and receiving the sort of adulation usually reserved for the top pop and movie stars. There is no transfer system between clubs and consequently each player signs a contract, usually for three years. This often leads to cloak-and-dagger situations especially during the final months of a player's agreement. Officially, it is illegal to approach a player until he has played his last game with a club, but it is not unusual to see Rugby League superstars being wined and dined by agents supposedly not connected with any club! Termination of contract makes the player a free agent and enables him to negotiate with any club for whatever fee he demands. At the same time all top players sign agreements enabling them to receive a signing-on fee each year before they even pass a ball. It is quite common for the top players to pick up a signing-on fee equivalent to £20,000 and then to receive an extra £250 for a win, £125 for a draw and £50 for a defeat.

With the advent of sponsorship and the huge amounts that clubs can earn from the one-armed bandit poker machines, the Australian Rugby League player is able to pick up more and more money. Yet, at the same time, some clubs still find it hard to keep paying top players large amounts.

Manly, who in recent years have signed many international players including England stars Mal Reilly, Phil Lowe and John Gray, get more than £250,000 towards the running of the club plus sponsorship worth £50,000. On the other side of the coin, Western Suburbs receive only £50,000 from their parent Leagues Club and players are forced to leave when chasing big contracts. Two years ago, Wests lost four top internationals – Tommy Raudonikis, Les Boyd, John Dorahy and Ray Brown – to rival clubs.

The Sydney Big League is undoubtedly the toughest competition in the world. It comprises twelve teams – St George, Manly-Warringah, North Sydney, South Sydney, Eastern Suburbs, Western Suburbs, Canterbury-Bankstown, Penrith, Cronulla-Sutherland, Parramatta, Balmain and Newtown. Each team plays each other twice and the top five compete in a play-off. Teams finishing in fourth and fifth place meet each other, the losers dropping out of the competition. The teams placed second and third clash and the winners gain the right to play the team which finished in top position.

38

28. Centre sensation Steve Rogers in goal-kicking action for Australia on their 1978 Tour.

Now it gets complicated! The losers (of the second-third play-off) meet the winners of the fourth-fifth game. The winners of the game between the top team and the winners of the second-third place play-off go through into the Grand Final.

The losers still live to fight another day; they play the victors of the game between the winners of the game between the fourth and fifth placed sides and the losers of the game between the second and third placed sides in the Minor Premiership Final for the right to go into the Grand Final.

Perhaps the following hypothetical table and results will help unravel the mysteries of the Sydney Premiership:

The top five positions:
1st   St George
2nd   Manly
3rd   Parramatta
4th   Easts
5th   Wests
First match – Easts 10 Wests 7
Second match – Manly 6 Parramatta 18
Third match – St George 12 Parramatta 10
St George go into the Grand Final
Fourth match – Manly 8 Easts 6
Fifth match (Minor Premiership Final) – Manly 11 Parramatta 18
Parramatta go into the Grand Final
Grand Final – St George 14 Parramatta 10

Easy, wasn't it?

The Sydney League also holds a knock-out competition played mid-week under lights at Balmain's home ground, Leichardt Oval, but this contest pales into insignificance compared with the Premiership. Very few games had been played under lights before its introduction in 1974 and it posed new problems for the players.

American training techniques have become commonplace in the Premiership, but one of them, the use of mascara spread under the eyes to prevent glare from the flood-lights, caused a great deal of amusement when top coach, Jack Gibson, sent out his he-men heroes looking more like half-dressed Al Jolsons than rough and tough rugby players. This technique also caused a few raised eyebrows among the British players during a match on their disastrous 1979 tour of Australia.

But the use of mascara is nothing in comparison with one incident recalled by British international hooker Mick Stephenson, who spent five years playing top grade Australian football following his then world record £20,000 transfer from the little Yorkshire club, Dewsbury, to Sydney giants Penrith. Stephenson remembers: 'In only my second game with Penrith I found myself changing next to our full-back Phil Jelay. Phil started to unravel a pair of the sexiest black hosiery one could ever wish to see and, with the artistry of a surgeon, he delicately cut away the legs and proceeded to step into the remains with the grace of a ballet dancer.

'Needless to say, I backed off to another part of the dressing room convinced that not all Aussies were big and strong. "I'm playing with a raving puff," I thought. Thankfully

40

29. Canterbury–Bankstown prop forward Geoff Robinson, known in the Sydney Big League as the 'Mountain Man' for his hairy look.

it quickly became evident that there was nothing queer about the wearing of panty hose – it cuts down on grass and scrub burns from the normally hard grounds.'

There was definitely nothing queer about another of Stephenson's Penrith colleagues. During a match against South Sydney a husky second row forward struck up a conversation with his opposite number, questioning his girlfriend's sexual expertise. Stephenson explains: 'The conversation had the desired result for it put their star player completely off his game. As captain I was overjoyed and we went in at half-time with a commanding lead.

'At the interval I congratulated our man for his astute use of on-field psychology.

'He replied, "Psychology my a———! I've been seeing his woman for more than three months."

' "What he doesn't know . . .," I replied with a wink. But one minute into the second half our lover boy was carried off. I felt the draught of the punch as it passed my ear in the scrum. It was right on target and he went out like a light. Apparently, on the morning of the game the lady in question had confessed all.'

The Sydney League produces its own brand of problems. There is so much pressure on everyone connected with the game. Coaches are classed as important as the players, and in some cases they receive even more cash than their stars who work with them. All clubs have their own video team which enables the coach to assess the failures or successes of each individual player for each match. Tackle counts, dropped balls, missed tackles, out-of-position and so on are all recorded and discussed with each player in the squad at training sessions. Players also have to watch a video recording of the previous week's game and of their opponents for the following weekend.

Players are thoroughly checked by club doctors who ensure that they are not 'carrying' any injury before training sessions begin. All clubs employ a specialised trainer and, under the guidance of the coach, he goes through a routine consisting of aerobics, callisthenics, weights and sprinting. Sessions last around three hours and each player is weighed after each run. During the week each player will also go through his own scaled training routine at home for about an hour a day and, as the weekend game gets closer, there are exercise sessions of two hours, practice of planned moves and motivation schemes.

Coaches keep a strict control. Late nights and drinking are banned for four days before a match and clubs have, in the past, fined players for breaking these stringent rules. Such is the speed of Sydney football that no team can afford to be anything but 100 per cent fit; after the final games late in September clubs take their squads overseas for an end-of-season wind-down. Hawaii, the American mainland, Bali, Fiji, and Thailand are just a few of the exotic places clubs visit to get away from it all. Not every club can finish the season in such style. Bottom of the league clubs often stay at home!

October is a rest time for the players. But in mid-November clubs usually call for once-a-week training sessions up until Christmas, and from the New Year three nights a week hard training is put in until the start of the pre-season competition during the first week of March.

Paying players big money for such demanding pressures does not mean the stars are always treated like royalty – far from it. Each player has to buy his own boots, shoulder pads and jockstraps; and clean them! Although jerseys are cleaned by the clubs, players must take care of their own shorts and socks. One club was forced to change the colour of its strip because of this ruling. Four players, all living together in a rented clubhouse,

42

decided to get a girl friend to wash their gear. Reluctantly, the girl dumped the kit in the washing machine without first checking its contents, which included one bright red towel. What a field day the Press and TV had when several players with the Penrith Panthers ran out for a match wearing pink shorts and socks! Penrith have since changed their strip from white to brown – and ordered players to beware of bright red towels.

Such light relief often breaks the intense pressure of the Big League. Different players have a wide range of activities to get away from the steamy cauldron of life in the Premiership. Many stars play the horses for relaxation; the more successful the horse, the better they play. One of Mick Stephenson's team mates, a flashing winger, went missing during the interval of a vital Premiership game. Hurriedly, a search party gathered and eventually found the player sitting in a toilet listening to a transistor radio for the result of the four o'clock. He promised to make amends in the second half, but fifteen minutes after the re-start he had done exactly the opposite – dropped balls, missed tackles and was a complete nervous wreck. Then he dropped to his knees after a weak tackle and the trainer was called on. Miraculously, he recovered in seconds to score a try and set up two other touchdowns and clinch a victory just as his team seemed to be heading for defeat. Later it was revealed that the trainer had told the player his nag had come home in the last race and he had picked up more than 500 dollars.

Gambling can be habit forming, but even worse, so can drugs. The very mention of the word in sporting circles creates an outcry. But, sad to say, they are used in Australia – and among Rugby League players. Mick Stephenson admits: 'I have taken drugs on many occasions, especially when I was struggling to hide an injury.

'They pay good money in Australia, but they also want their pound of flesh. Some players will do practically anything to get out onto the field of play.

'My club, Penrith, never gave me any drugs at all during my playing career. But I did buy them myself and took them without Penrith knowing. I couldn't say one way or another if other players did the same, but I have seen a fair share of opponents packing down against me with glazed eyes that certainly didn't come from wintergreen or rubbing oil.'

The physiotherapist at Penrith certainly knew how to get the best out of drugs. Stevo explains: 'Playing in a semi-final always needs that little extra and the physio gave us just that. Craftily going among the players just before the kick-off he handed out "something special".

' "It won't harm you – but watch it boost your game," he said to each player in turn.

'I'd already "popped" my own brand of booster and was a little wary of over-doing it, so I put the pill in my pocket. We won the match convincingly with every player turning in a star performance.

'The following week I remembered the pill and took it to a chemist for analysis. Barely two minutes later he returned with the dramatic revelation: "It's a salt tablet!" That's psychology for you!'

Like the clubs and the players the crowd also adopt a 'win at all costs' attitude. Redfern Oval, home of South Sydney, has a band of fans that are unique in Australian Rugby League. As Mick Stephenson explains: 'The Redfern Oval is in the Aboriginal area of Sydney, the Aborigines are proud of their heritage and, on occasions, they have been known to take a drink or two. One group used to amaze me with their humour, especially if we were lined up behind the goal line awaiting a penalty kick.

'During one match one of these Aborigines decided to "point the bone" at me, something similar to sticking pins in dolls. I laughingly scoffed at the thought. Just two minutes later I was carried off after ripping my cartilage. I never scoffed after that.'

Despite the intense pressure on all Australian Rugby League players everybody has got to learn and certainly young Ross Gigg learned the hard way. While playing for Penrith against Manly Ross took the ball from the kick-off and surged downfield on a great weaving run, before collapsing without a finger being laid on him. He was carried off with a suspected broken leg and yet, when his team-mates went to the dressing room at half-time, Ross was sitting on a bench, his face as red as a beetroot and holding a stud spanner in his hand. Believe it or not he'd put his boot on with the spanner still inside!

Yet nobody can laugh at the all-conquering Australians. They do rule supreme and, unless the rest of the Rugby League playing nations adopt a far more professional approach to the game, it is going to be a long, long time before the Kangaroos are deposed.

Britain may have the more skilful players, but the Australians have the fitness and power to overwhelm the opposition.

CHAPTER FOUR

Pushing back the frontiers

Rugby League in France has faced crisis upon crisis – many inflicted by their own countrymen's hot-blooded and reckless temperament. Violence in international matches in France has reached such a state that the European Championship tournament between teams from England, Wales and France, and representative games between Great Britain and France at under-24 and under-19 Colts level were thrown in jeopardy. Only top level talks in London between leading officials from Britain and France eased the situation.

A three point plan was issued: 'Referees in international matches from now on are ordered to dismiss players from the field immediately for any act of violence; each visiting country will provide the referee and one touch judge, who will be a senior referee; a four-man committee will be drawn up, two from each country, with the away side providing the chairman which will be present at every European match with powers to sit immediately after the game to consider the case of any dismissed players. Any ban imposed by the committee, however, will be at international level and will not affect a player's club career.'

The situation reached crisis point in early 1980 when, after England had beaten France 4–2 in an ugly match, the England team and Huddersfield referee Billy Thompson were locked in their dressing rooms for an hour to protect them from angry French supporters. Ironically, the English players spent their time in the dressing rooms – playing charades!

Yet, even the sight of French supporters baying for the blood of the English players paled somewhat compared with the notorious 'Battle of Albi' in 1976. That match, between Great Britain under-24s and France, was nothing more than a running battle as the French, aided by the referee, tried everything – including kicking, biting and scratching – to win. British prop John Wood was rushed to hospital and had to stay there for several days with a head injury and following the game one of the French players, Marcel Charcos, and referee André Lacaze were banned for life. The suspension was later lifted.

It was rough play that partly led to the formation of Rugby League in France. At the beginning of 1931 the four British members of the Home Rugby Union Championship banned the French from the competition because of alleged professionalism and rough play. The ban from the fifteen-a-side code left the door wide open for Rugby League to be introduced in France. An exhibition match was fixed up between the touring Australians and Great Britain to be played in Paris on 31 December 1933. The Australians raced to an impressive 63–13 victory.

Among the pioneers was a Frenchman Jean Galia, a Villeneuve and Toulouse centre

30. The French line-up for the deciding match in Narbonne for the European Championship.

who had made many Rugby Union international appearances. Galia persuaded sixteen of his Union colleagues to try their hand at the League game and they made a tour of England in 1934. Although the French side won only one of their six matches – that against Hull – they were hooked on the sport. On 2 April of that year the Fédération Français de Jeu à Treize was officially formed and thirteen days later they staged their first international, against England at Buffalo Vellodrome in Paris, a game the English won 32–21.

The French League competition began the following October with twelve founder member clubs – Albi, Bordeaux, Côte Basque, Grenoble, La Rochelle, Lyons, Paris Celtic, Pau, Roanne, S. O. Béziers, Sport Olympique de Paris and Villeneuve-sur-Lot. During that first season Salford and Hunslet made short tours of France, and Villeneuve, led by Galia, played exhibition matches at Warrington, Broughton, Hull, Oldham and Leeds – losing them all.

The French received a tremendous boost on New Year's Day 1935 when they recorded their first international triumph, beating Wales 18–11 at Bordeaux. Four years later the French had taken to the game so well that they lifted the European International Championship for the first time. Little did they realise then that a major setback was just around the corner. Two years after the outbreak of the Second World War the German-backed Vichy Government of Marshal Henri Philippe Petain banned the game.

The proclamation read: 'Secretary of State for National Education and Youth. No. 5285 – Decree of the 19th December 1941, bringing about the dissolution of the Association called French League of Rugby XIII. We, the Field Marshal of France, the head of the French State, in view of the law on the 20th December 1940 relating to sporting organisation, in view of the proposal of the Secretary of State for National Education of Youth decree:

'First Article – The Association called French League of Rugby XIII whose offices are at 24 Rue Drouot, Paris is dissolved, assent having been refused it.

'Second Article – The patrimony (property and money) of the Association dissolved by virtue of the preceding article, is transferred, without modification, to the National Committee of Sports who assume all its charges and will be represented in the operation of liquidation by its secretary-general M. Charles Denis.

46

31. New Zealand skipper Roy Christian is chaired by his victorious team mates following the Kiwis' 1971 Test series triumph in Britain. Roy is a descendant of Fletcher Christian of 'Mutiny on the Bounty' fame.

32. The 1980 New Zealand tourists perform their traditional Haka – the Maori war dance – before the First Test at Wigan which they drew 14–14.

'Third Article – The Secretary of State for National Education, Youth and Sports is charged with the execution of this present decree which will be published in the official journal. Made at Vichy, 29th December 1941.'

Despite the decree Rugby League continued to be played in villages situated well away from hostile German eyes. At the end of the war the French began a massive rebuilding operation but were ready to welcome an English team to Paris in January 1946.

France's best years came at the end of the forties and in the early fifties when they carried off the European Championship against England and Wales in three successive seasons. The French made their first tour of Australia and New Zealand in 1951, beating the Australians 2–1 in the test series and losing their one test in New Zealand. They repeated the feat against Australia in 1955 and in 1960 they drew the series after one win each and an 8–8 draw. The French's international success in the early fifties led to the first World Cup being staged in France in 1954, a championship won by Dave Valentine's gallant British squad.

During the last twenty years Rugby League in France has fluctuated between the dizzy heights of international success and the dark depths of despair, as the game has been rocked by a succession of trials and tribulations both on and off the field. Several times French referees have been openly accused of being biased in favour of their own countrymen. French officials have actually 'shown the flag' during an international match against England at Narbonne in 1980, when their touch judges ran the line carrying flags bearing the rallying call, 'Allez France'.

Referees have been known to disallow perfectly legal tries by the opposition while disregarding infringements by Frenchmen who have gone on to score tries. In one amazing incident at the Parc de Princes in Paris when France was playing Britain, a French winger raced behind a touch judge and onto the cycle track before running back onto the field and touching down for a remarkable try – which the referee allowed! One referee, Michel Sagoty, introduced his own 'sin-bin' in an under-24 international

48

against Great Britain. He sent British hooker Graham Liptrot of St Helens to the side-lines for ten minutes to cool off. It was left to British League secretary David Oxley to rush onto the field and inform Sagoty that such a ruling was not covered by inter-national laws. Liptrot returned to the field and Britain won the match.

The passion for the game in France is such that it will survive come what may! The international side invariably provides a feast of attacking skills, although their lack of discipline and hot-headed temperament often lets them down on the big occasion.

The story in New Zealand, where Rugby League is played on a strictly amateur level, is similar to France in that it is overshadowed by the strength and success of their Rugby Union counterparts. The New Zealand All Blacks are, arguably, the best international Rugby Union side in the world and, consequently, the Kiwis play a minor role in the sporting life of that country. Although New Zealand is the most amateur of the world's Rugby League nations their first squad to tour Australia and England in 1907 was sarcastically dubbed the 'All Golds' – because they were going to play for money! Two years earlier winger George W. Smith, who toured England with the New Zealand Rugby Union squad, met several Northern Union officials and players and agreed to consider a suggestion that he should assemble a party of players and return to England to undertake a tour as professionals. On his arrival back in New Zealand, Smith discussed the idea with Albert Henry Baskerville, a forward with Wellington's Oriental Rugby Union Club. Baskerville and Smith made plans for the 1907 trip and such was the feeling in New Zealand against professional sport that, when the tourists accepted an offer to play three matches in Sydney on their way to England, jeering crowds lined the docks as their ship sailed away. The tourists received a £500 guarantee for the three matches and part of that money was allocated to take the brilliant Australian, H. H. 'Dally' Messenger, on the tour.

The All Golds won all three matches in Sydney – fifteen-a-side under Union rules – against New South Wales. The tourists arrived in England on 30 September 1907 and were scheduled to play an incredible thirty-five games. Even more amazing was the fact that of the 27-strong party, only Smith knew anything about Northern Union laws. Even so, the tourists won nineteen of their matches, scoring 414 points and conceding 294 and their greatest achievement came in their first internationals when, despite vast inexperience, they managed to win the Test series 2–1 against the Northern Union. During the tour, in November 1907, the New Zealand Rugby Union declared the All Golds 'professional' and suspended them. On their way home the All Golds stopped off in Australia to play their first Test series against the Kangaroos, winning two of the matches and drawing the other.

The following year the native Maoris, who took to Rugby League like ducks to water, sent a touring team to Australia where one of the great favourites of the party was Opai Asher, a winger, who used to leap over opponents to beat tackles.

The outbreak of War saw the cancellation of tours until 1919 and history was made three years later when New Zealand received a visit from the Australian Universities. The game progressed steadily up to the Second World War and the outbreak of hostilities in September 1939 cost the New Zealanders £8,000 – the cost of sending a touring team to Britain to play just two matches before war was declared.

The Kiwis gained one of their greatest triumphs in 1952 when they won all three Test matches against Australia, but it was nineteen years later when they found themselves

33. St Helens skipper Len Aston (centre) meets Italian captain Bartolotto before a friendly match at Knowsley Road in 1950 during Italy's brief courtship with the game of Rugby League.

really 'on top of the world'. After beating Australia 24–3 in the mud of Auckland's Carlaw Park they travelled to Britain to win the Test series 2–1, and followed that up by winning two of their three Tests in France and drawing the other one.

Because the game in New Zealand is now purely amateur some of their greatest stars have pursued their Rugby League careers in Australia and Britain. Sydney club Canterbury Bankstown signed centre Bernie Lowther and packman Henry Tatana after that 1971 tour, while a good many years earlier Cec Mountford played in England with Wigan.

There has been a striking expansion of Rugby League in New Zealand over the last few years and now most of the country's major universities play the game alongside Leagues from Auckland, Canterbury, Gisbourne-East, Coast Bays, Hawkes Bay, Midlands Bay of Plenty and Manawatu.

Apart from the leading Rugby League nations of Britain, Australia, France and New Zealand, plus the bubbling new 'babe' of Papua New Guinea, the game has, in its time, also caught the imagination of sporting enthusiasts in Italy, Yugoslavia and America. In the fifties there were great hopes that Rugby League would become established in Italy where amateur sides had been formed. Italian teams made short tours of England in 1950 and 1954, on the later trip taking part in a triangular international tournament at amateur level. Unfortunately, they were beaten 20–6 by France at Huddersfield and 18–11 by England at Halifax.

Financial help was given to the Italians by the English Rugby League and at one time there were more than twenty clubs playing the game in places such as Milan, Turin and Venice. Italian Toni Rossi was a popular forward with Wigan in the early sixties, earning a first team place after writing to Central Park and asking for a trial. In 1960 the Australian World Cup team played three games in Italy while several amateur sides from both France and England have visited the land of spaghetti and vino.

50

Rugby League was played in Yugoslavia in the fifties as a result of visits by French amateur sides. The country was represented at a meeting of the International Board held in Paris during October 1954 when the first World Cup series was played. Milan Kosanovic, who was born in Yugoslavia and went to England as a boy, was a member of Wakefield Trinity's Challenge Cup-winning team at Wembley in 1963 when they beat Wigan 25–10.

The first Rugby League games to be played in America were staged in November 1954 when the Australian and New Zealand World Cup team played each other in two games at Long Beach Memorial Stadium and the Coliseum in Los Angeles – both in California, the heartland of Rugby Union in America. The attendances were affected by fog, and only 1,000 fans turned up to 'see' Australia win the first game 30–13. Australia were victors in the second game 28–18 before a crowd of 4,554.

A year earlier a team of grid-iron footballers had made a Rugby League tour of Australia and New Zealand. Billed as the 'American All Stars' they played twenty-six matches, winning three of their eighteen games in Australia and four of their matches in New Zealand. The Americans were given some preliminary coaching by Cliff Evans who played Rugby League with Leeds and Salford. Later on that year an American Rugby League team played five matches in France, winning just one. At that time France was celebrating the twentieth anniversary of the game's introduction and three of the Americans played in a special match in which France defeated a Rest of the World team 19–15. Ironically, the 'World' side included an Italian, Vigna, who scored a try, as well as British and Australian players.

Twenty years later, grid-iron star and Wisconsin businessman, Mike Mayer, became hooked on the game after seeing the Richard Harris film, 'This Sporting Life', on television. The film was based on life in the raw and centred around a Rugby League side. Mayer saw the potential of establishing the game in America and formed the United States Rugby League, installing himself as president. The four world powers gave official blessing to the USRL and Britain dipped deep into her cash reserves with loans exceeding £25,000. Plans to stage exhibition matches in the summer of 1980 collapsed when Mayer failed to find a guarantor.

If Rugby League is to conquer more countries it is essential the game becomes established in the United States where it would become the springboard for launching the game in the Far East.

CHAPTER FIVE

Characters and comedians

The Rugby League abounds with stories funny and curious. Many are fictional, some apocryphal, a few are fact. Here we have gathered a varied selection – some old, some new, some borrowed, some blue. Some are brave enough to put their names to the stories; in other cases we have left the names in the dug-out – to protect the guilty.

Big Jim Mills, the giant Welsh prop, has the unenviable record of being sent off more times than any other player in the history of the game. He is one of rugby's greatest and most controversial characters and is under a lifetime ban by the New Zealand authorities following an incident during a Wales–Kiwi World Championship clash in Swansea in 1975. Yet off the field he is one of the game's most likeable personalities, often breaking into song to entertain team mates and fans and always ready and willing to relate a fund of funny stories – many of them taking the mickey out of himself.

On arriving in Queensland with the British tourists in 1979, Australian photographers wanted shots of eighteen-stone Big Jim in some kind of action. He duly obliged by lifting the rear end of a conveniently parked mini car. It was a feat he performed many times on the tour, but on one occasion it wasn't for the eyes of the Press alone.

During a stay in Sydney, ever-joking Jim lifted a mini and wheeled it 200 yards down the road. He was spotted by policemen in a patrol car which, blue lights flashing, screeched to a halt alongside the latest-style wheelbarrow!

'Come on Jim,' said a burly bobby in blue, 'put it back!'

The local Romeo, who regularly parked his vehicle outside his girlfriend's home, doesn't know to this day how come the next morning it was parked the other way round. Ask Jim!

Tours invariably bring out the best and the funniest in players. Team mates of Big Jim on that 1979 tour were mini half-back masters Steve Nash and Roger Millward. Early on in the trip both players were struck down by cartilage injuries. Both limped badly and both had to walk with the aid of walking sticks. On one evening, as the two players relaxed in a bar, their injured legs propped up on stools, an old black and white mongrel hobbled into the hotel.

'Look at that,' said Millward to Nash, 'even the dogs are taking the mickey.'

Then there was the story of the British forward who took tea with a rather shapely lady one evening. The pair were getting to know each other better when there came the sound of a key being turned in the front door lock.

'What's that?' he cried.

'It's my husband. He's early!'

'Where's the back door?' asked our over-friendly forward, hastily adjusting his tie.

'We haven't got one,' she replied.

Came the retort: 'Where do you want one?'

On the World Cup trip to Australia and New Zealand in 1978 the British party were treated to two days in the paradise world of Queensland's Magnetic Island. The sun blazed down, the blue sea quietly lapped the white sand on the shore. No training for the players, no work for the Press – it was heaven on earth. Soon after the boat docked, one member of the party complained bitterly: 'What the hell have we come here for? It's like a bloody concentration camp!'

Jim Hoey was one of the great second row forwards with Widnes during the twenties and early thirties. For more than a decade he delighted the fans with his happy-go-lucky manner, his remarkable skills and his scoring feats. Like Rugby League itself stories involving Hoey are legion – here are a couple of them.

Playing against Leeds in the 1927–8 season, Widnes were losing 9–7 with only minutes remaining. A long kick down field by Leeds eventually found its way to Hoey on the touchline. Off went Jimmy on a galloping run. On the half-way line he sold a dummy to beat a cover tackler and then, on the Leeds 25, another Leeds defender was left stranded. As he went for the corner, three Leeds defenders closed in. Watching Hoey's amazing run on the touchline was a burly 17-stone police constable, wearing a regulation white mackintosh and size eleven boots. As the defenders moved in, Hoey sold his final outrageous dummy and the three tacklers piled into the bobby – leaving Hoey to touch down for a winning try.

Five years later Hoey created Rugby League history by becoming the first player to appear and score in every match for his club in one season.

The last Widnes match of that season was away at Barrow. The home skipper, Bill Burgess, approached Jimmy before the match and jokingly said: 'Let us win and we'll give you a goal.' The irrepressible Jimmy retorted, 'Don't worry Bill. I'll get one without help from you!' In fact, he didn't score a goal. Widnes won with three tries – all scored by Hoey!

Another goalkicker, who was a colourful character, was French international full-back Puig Aubert, one of his country's greatest players. It is said that during club matches in the South of France, while his side was attacking and he could relax, he would wander over to the sideline and beg a cigarette from one of his fans, take a couple of puffs and then return to the action.

Kevin Ashcroft and Alex Murphy, who played in highly-successful sides at Leigh and Warrington and were again paired at Salford, Alex as coach, Kevin as hooker, were a lively double act in English Rugby League. They were once charged with bringing the game into disrepute following their antics during the interval at a televised Floodlit Trophy match at Leigh; at the time Rugby League commentator Eddie Waring was particularly popular with his 'It's A Knockout' programme. As the teams emerged for the second half Alex and Kevin brought out a huge, six foot card depicting a Joker. The crowd loved it. Rugby League officials didn't.

Murphy, the supreme joker, gave his own style of award to players while he was coaching at Leigh. As training came to a close every Tuesday and Thursday, players would anxiously watch as Murphy disappeared down the tunnel to engrave the night's trophy – for the worst player. That trophy was a rusty, old dustbin lid.

Much earlier in his career, Murphy, then a St Helens star, was doing his National Service with the RAF. Inevitably, he became involved in Rugby Union and took part in

34. Big Jim Mills with another famous superstar – three-times Grand National winner Red Rum.

35. The other side of Big Jim Mills, showing the aggression that made him one of the most feared forwards in the game.

inter-service matches. Murphy only knows how to play rugby one way – to win. That is how he played it one midweek afternoon, breaking the nose of his opposite number in a particularly rugged tackle. It was only later, when he was mysteriously put on jankers, that he discovered the player was due to play for England in a championship match the following Saturday.

To be a top prop, players don't necessarily need a high IQ, a point underlined when one such forward filled in his injury claims form.

Departmental position: Open side prop
Clock number: Eight

The figure which proved too much for Roy Baira of the Brisbane Natives club was ninety-nine. That was the number of years for which he was banned after being charged with assaulting a referee. Later, the Appeals Board lopped eighty-nine years off his sentence. Roy will be thirty-eight years old when he can resume rugby in 1990.

36. Harold Wagstaff, who led Britain to that historic 'Rorke's Drift' Test triumph.

One player who was felled in a match was St Helens loose forward Harry Pinner. He stayed down as if he had breathed his last, but the referee, waving the sponge man away, soon had him back in action. 'Come on, Harry,' he said, 'stay down there much longer and you'll get sunburned!'

The word 'fan' came into use around the turn of the century, soon after the birth of the thirteen-a-side code. It is an abbreviation of 'fantastic' – literally one who is possessed of the enthusiasm or madness of the temple engendered by over-indulgence in religious rites.

There are twin temples in the rugby-mad city of Kingston-upon-Hull where fan fever is not simply a religious rite – it's a way of life. Hull is a divided city: to the East is the temple of Craven Park, home of Hull Kingston Rovers; to the West lies the Boulevard, home of Hull. Two Rugby League sides separated by a few miles, a metropolis of modern shops and an eternity of enmity.

Hull Kingston Rovers to the East, Hull to the West – and ne'er the twain shall meet. Not, that is, unless it is in combat and then the meeting is head on with no quarter given or asked. Rovers play in red and white, Hull in black and white. They are emotive colours on Humberside. They make some folk see red, or give black looks. All depending on which side of the fence you were born.

A 'mixed marriage' on Humberside relates to the wedding between a boy from the Boulevard and a girl from Hull Kingston Rovers – or vice-versa. Such associations are frowned upon as unholy alliances. Another union given the elbow on Humberside is bacon-and-eggs! No true Boulevard fan will ever admit to eating such food, for red and white is a hated combination. Over on the other side of the city, no self-respecting child would dream of eating humbugs. Not that he would find such a sweet in any shop around Craven Park.

Fan fever goes back through the history of sport. In the years before the wireless came into general use, and before we could depend on a rapid results service, Northern fans used pigeons to carry news of their favourites away from their own midden. Fans travelling to away matches would often take with them assorted shoe boxes complete with air holes. Inside were their pet homing pigeons prepared for the flight back home. At half-time and full-time the pigeons would be freed carrying with them the scores and brief details about the match.

56

37. St Helens loose-forward Harry Pinner breaks from a scrum to be met by Wakefield Trinity's ex-Rugby Union international Mike Lampkowski.

It's the immediacy of modern radio which is so appealing to fans, but it has its drawbacks too. That noted commentator, Keith Macklin, recalls a match he covered at Craven Park where Hull Kingston Rovers were playing Leigh – in the fog. So bad was visibility that Keith was unable to see more than half the field. Like a true professional he got on with the job working by the programme in front of him and listening for crowd reaction when play was lost in the swirling fog. When there were cheers, Hull K.R. were in the ascendancy; boos and catcalls meant Leigh were getting the better of the exchanges.

Keith recalls: 'It went well and Ted Brophy, the Leigh prop, had a blinder. I said so – many times.' The problem was Ted wasn't playing. He had been replaced before the match: no one had told Keith to amend his programme. Ted Brophy didn't mind. He claimed wages and expenses for playing. 'Of course I played,' he insisted. 'Didn't you hear Keith Macklin on the radio!'

One team was once given a no-nonsense choice – expenses or a fish and chip supper. The Yorkshire side was returning home from an 'A' team fixture when the hard-up committee gave them the option: '2s 6d in your pocket or fish 'n' chips in your stomach?'

One foodshop proprietor and staunch Rochdale Hornets' fan offered to provide

38. It's K–9! It was the black-and-white mongrel dog which evaded capture by players, officials and police during a televised cup tie between Leeds and Halifax, much to the amusement of the Headingley crowd and millions of TV viewers. Our picture shows K–9 preparing to tackle snow-bound Leeds winger John Atkinson.

nourishment to one star winger from the Athletic Ground. Wickham J. Powell was, apparently, not being given enough chances by his inside colleagues. The following week the outraged shopkeeper displayed the following notice in his window: 'If the Hornets won't feed Wick Powell, we will!'

A team mate of Powell's at Rochdale, one Joe Bowers, was given the ball during the match and scored a spectacular try, only to have it disallowed. The ball burst when he touched down.

Some of the best Rugby League stories today are the ones that have been handed down through the mists of time. One involves a struggling Rugby League team that was playing so badly that gates dwindled to a mere trickle and even the handful of fans that did turn up were able to wander in without paying. One fan, obviously plagued by his conscience, sent the admission money to the club treasurer. Back came the reply, 'Thank you for the money, which player do you want to buy.'

There is also the story of the player – probably from the same struggling side – who was in grave danger of losing his place because of a string of poor performances. The club coach had tried all he knew to try and improve the form of the player, but to no avail. Eventually one fan recommended the coach to feed him black puddings and pigs' trotters. Almost in despair the coach bought 15 lbs of black puddings and 20 lbs of pigs' trotters. On his way back to the ground the coach stopped for a chat with a rival team boss.

'What have you got there?' he asked.

'Fifteen pounds of black puddings and 20 lbs of pigs' trotters for that No. 8 of ours.'

'You've got a good deal there,' came the smart reply.

In the early seventies many English clubs struggled to survive financially, Bank accounts were overdrawn and monthly statements were opened in fear. One First Division secretary, who wishes to remain anonymous for obvious reasons, paid a visit to his local bank and presented a cheque to be cashed for the players' wages.

'We had such a big overdraft that the manager fell about laughing,' said the secretary. 'Tears were rolling down his cheeks, he was laughing that much. It was only because he had a sense of humour that we actually got the money.'

Then there's the story involving Mick Stephenson during his Australian days. Stevo was hit in a rather painful place as he was tackled. On came the trainer with a cold sponge and pushed it down the front of his shorts. Mick yelled with pain and shouted: 'Don't rub 'em – count 'em.'

Rugby League is justly proud of its image as a rugged game played in a sporting tradition – rigidly refereed by men who have the respect of players – but, like any bodily contact sport, clashes with authority come quick and fast. Players know who's boss – but what the boss doesn't know . . .

It was the Third Test at Leeds in 1978, Australia were home and dry and the final minutes were ticking away; Jim Mills and Aussie loose forward Ray Price were involved in a tackle. The ball was played and play went on. 'Should I hit him?' thought Jim. 'Aye, why not.' And he did!

The touch judge raced on to reveal all to referee Mick Naughton of Widnes. Mick called Big Jim over. 'I saw that,' he said.

'I bet he didn't,' replied Jim.

Playing in front of the Thre'penny Stand at the Boulevard, Hull can be a hair-raising experience for players not wearing the familiar black and white strip. An international class wingman, rather dark in complexion, had a nightmare match on one occasion at the Boulevard. He dropped passes and missed tackles throughout the first half. The second half began no better. His side was attacking, the ball was whisked across the line and finally was swept along to him. He missed it, the ball hit him on the head and bounced into touch. One wag in the Thre'penny Stand shouted: 'In off black, seven away!'

One of Britain's popular forwards is pig farmer, newsagent and Huyton player-coach Geoff Fletcher. Geoff is a realist: 'Huyton aren't the best team in the league,' he says. They were playing at Alt Park and losing by the odd forty points to champions-elect Featherstone Rovers. Downhearted? Not Geoff! As he and his team stood behind the posts and Rovers' kicker Steve Quinn set up another goal, Geoff could clearly be heard to rally his men saying: 'Come on, we can beat this load of rubbin' rags!'

It was in the same match that one of Geoff's team mates was heard to mutter one or two unkind words about a touch judge. The aforesaid official overheard the remark and called over referee Stan Wall of Leigh. 'He called me a "stupid jerk" [or words to that effect],' said the indignant official. Mr Wall called Geoff Fletcher and the guilty player to heel and the player apologised.

Featherstone's Steve Quinn took the resultant penalty. One touch judge raised his flag to signal success, the other kept his down, signalling failure. Mr Fletcher approached Mr Wall. 'I can't say much for the lad,' said Mr Fletcher. 'But he is right about that touch judge, he *is* a stupid jerk.'

Leigh's international referee, Stan Wall, believes a referee must be prepared to match a player's banter. 'I have a running battle with Featherstone's Mick Morgan. In one match at Post Office Road, Mick was giving me earache. I called him over and said, "Hey Mick, I left my wife at home 'cos she was nagging; now I've got you." '

Sometimes it is the club officials who have the last laugh. Castleford centre Phil Johnson threatened to quit the game because his club wouldn't put him on the transfer list. Castleford chairman Gordon Appleyard explained: 'He was holding a gun at our heads, so I wished him a long and happy retirement.'

CHAPTER SIX

Great moments in Rugby League

In the annals of British military history the battle at Rorke's Drift in Zululand on 22 January 1879 ranks as one of the great rearguard actions of modern warfare. There, in the first month of the Zulu War two British officers – Lieutenants Chard and Bromhead – and about 150 men of the Royal Welch Fusiliers checked the frightening advance of some 10,000 warriors of the Zulu nation.

On that bloody day the gallant defenders won a magnificent victory and were later awarded eleven Victoria Crosses, the most given in any single action.

Thirty-five years later a slightly-built young man called Harold Wagstaff was to lead a second 'Rorke's Drift' rearguard action for Britain. The Third Test between Australia and Britain on 4 July 1914 will forever be known as the 'Rorke's Drift' Test. It was a Test of incredible endurance and courage, a desperate battle against all the odds in the cauldron of Sydney Cricket Ground in front of 34,420 partisan fans.

Britain, fighting for the Ashes, had been forced into playing three tests in eight days despite a growing casualty count. The squad had been crippled by injury and worse was to follow in that amazing Third Test.

For the full story we must first go back to the British captain, Harold Wagstaff – Waggy, the Huddersfield centre, and one of the greatest names the sport has seen. He was born in Underbank, Yorkshire, in 1891 and reputedly signed for Huddersfield for five gold sovereigns. He played his first match against Bramley at Barley Mow and went on to play in 474 games for the Claret and Golds.

Waggy became an international at seventeen, two years after signing for Huddersfield, and went on to captain Britain on two tours, 1914 and 1920. He was a player of remarkable ability, a graceful, try-making centre who could think, act and react in the blink of an eye. He was the master of the unorthodox, a fact underlined on that 1914 tour.

In one match, faced by a trio of Aussies, Waggy tossed the ball into the air. His opponents stopped in amazement and, in that stunning moment, Waggy caught the ball and, quick as a flash, ghosted past them and went over for a try. It was a moment of pure inspiration, a lighter moment on a tour which endeared Harold Wagstaff to the tough, sport-loving Australians for ever and showed to the world the true bulldog spirit of the British sportsman.

The tour itself began with an injury crisis – Waggy has since declared that the squad was not fully fit – and he ordered rigorous training in preparation for the First Test at the Agricultural Ground, Sydney, on 27 June. A crowd of 40,000 saw Britain win 23–5 despite playing Leeds forward Bill Jarman at full-back. Both the regular full-backs, Alf Wood (broken nose) and Gwyn Thomas (broken rib), were injured.

39. The 1956 Challenge Cup winners – St Helens, who included skipper Alan Prescott and coach Jim Sullivan.

The Second Test had been scheduled to be staged forty-eight hours later in honour of the King's Birthday. Excitement was at fever pitch as 55,000 fans crowded into Sydney Cricket Ground for the match, with Britain barely able to field a side because of further injuries to Bert Jenkins, Jarman and the Huddersfield pair, Longstaffe and Stan Moorhouse. At half-time it was 7–7 but Australia powered home in the second half to square the series with a 12–7 triumph.

Thus the scene was set for the 'Rorke's Drift' Test. The third match should have been played later in the tour, but Australia insisted it should be played the following Saturday in place of the scheduled match against New South Wales. British manager Mr J. Clifford rejected the proposal and the British squad went off to play a regional match against Western District at Bathurst, a match they won 42–3 in front of 1,200 fans who paid £51.

Meanwhile, the Australians were agitating for the Third Test to be played on the Saturday. They cabled officials in England and a specially convened Northern Union Council agreed to their demands. They sent their message by cable to British managers Mr Clifford and Mr J. Houghton. It read: 'Play match as Australians desire. England expects that every man will do his duty.' Britain prepared for the match and Alf Wood elected to play full-back despite his broken nose. The British side was: Wood; Williams, Hall, Wagstaff, Davies; Smith, Prosser; Holland, Coldrick, Ramsdale, Johnson, Clark and Chilcott.

The Aussies lined up: Hallett; Frawley, Deane, Tidyman, W. Messenger; Fraser, Halloway; Burge, Courtney, Craig, Sullivan, Pearce and Cann.

The thirteen British players were called into a room at the hotel for their pre-match talk. Mr Clifford gave a stirring speech, outlining the reasons for the switch and entreating all his men to play as they had never played before.

Harold Wagstaff later recalled, 'He told us we were playing a game of football that afternoon, but more than that – we were playing for England.

62

40. Don Fox, Wakefield Trinity's international pack star, hides his head in grief after missing an easy goal attempt – a goal that would have given his side Challenge Cup glory at Wembley during the 1968 final against Leeds. Instead Fox finished the afternoon in tears and Leeds collected the game's greatest prize.

'The men in my team were moved. I was impressed and thrilled as never before or since by a speech. You could see our fellows clenching their fists as Mr Clifford spoke. None of us said a word as we left that room.'

Britain walked right into more trouble when in the opening minutes of the match

41. The Odsal Stadium, Bradford, on the day 102,569 fans packed the ground for the 1954 Challenge Cup Final replay.

winger Frank Williams twisted his leg. Chick Johnson was taken from the pack to assist on the flanks. But British resolve and natural ability began to pay handsome dividends with some bright, attacking football and Waggy's heroes turned round 9–3 to the good, thanks to three Wood goals and a try from Percy Coldrick.

Soon after the restart Huddersfield forward Douglas Clark, who had broken a thumb in the first half and had it heavily bandaged so he could continue, fell heavily and smashed his collarbone. Twice he had it strapped, twice he tried to play on, but in the end the pain became unbearable. Tears welled in his eyes as he trudged away from the action. Shortly afterwards Williams hurt his leg again; this time he had to go off. Then Oldham centre Billy Hall was carried off with concussion. Britain were down to ten men and half an hour of the match remained.

Britain defended like lionhearts, pummelled into the ground but never into submission by the strong Australians. Then, at threequarter-time, Britain attacked. Waggy broke through and sent Chick Johnson in the clear. Johnson, a soccer man at heart, put boot to ball and dribbled it through the middle of the home defence for a sensational try. Australia never recovered; Britain won the 'Rorke's Drift' Test 14–6 – and the Ashes.

That magnificent 'Rorke's Drift' Test of 1914 will never be forgotten. It has been unequalled in the history of Rugby League. But in 1958, when Australia and Britain clashed in Test action yet again, there came another heroic display by British players.

The Australian Tour began against a backcloth of discontent with coach Jim Brough and managers Tom Mitchell and Bennett Manson coming down hard on discipline and imposing curfews. These measures did not go down well with the players, as was only too apparent during the First Test at Sydney on 14 June. Britain fumbled their way to

64

WARRINGTON RUGBY FOOTBALL CLUB

Back Row:—*E. White, S. Phillips, R. Ryan, G. Lowe, J. Challinor, A. Stevens, A. Humphreys, B. Bevan, H. Fishwick.*
Sitting:—*W. Sheridan, A. Heathwood, D. Naughton, S. McCormick, A. Naughton, C. Mountford, E. Frodsham, R. Ryder, H. Bath, F. Wright.*
Front:—*R. L. CHAMPIONSHIP CUP ; R. Price, R. L. CHALLENGE CUP ; G. Helme, LANCS. LEAGUE CUP.*

42. The victorious Warrington team following their epic triumph in the 1954 Cup Final replay at Odsal.

defeat by 25–8 and after that disaster the touring squad had a top secret meeting and thrashed out their disagreements.

The meeting obviously had the desired effect for Britain won all their 'country' matches and the scene was set for the Second Test, with the British squad training in the luxury and oppulence of Surfers' Paradise. The early-tour wrangles were forgotten and team spirit soared sky-high.

Gates were closed at the Brisbane Exhibition Ground with more than 37,000 packing the stadium and thousands more locked out.

Britain had to win to keep the series alive. The match kicked off amid extremes of excitement, but after only four minutes British skipper Alan Prescott fell awkwardly in a tackle and broke his right arm. Prop forward Alan told his team mates, 'I've broken my arm. Protect me – but don't let on.' Despite such a shattering blow Britain scored a try through centre Jim Challinor and were leading when they were rocked by another cruel twist of fate. Stand-off Dave Bolton was sent crashing to the ground by a fierce tackle and was taken to hospital with a fractured collarbone, an injury which ended his tour.

Britain, with only eleven fit men and with Eric Fraser, Vince Karalius and Challinor badly knocked about, still dominated the match and went in at half-time leading 10–2. The English dressing room at the interval resembled a scene from Emergency Ward Ten on a really bad night. A doctor firmly advised Prescott to stay off the field and warned him if he continued he could do irreparable damage to his arm. Prescott would have none of it, saying: 'My place is on the field – we've got to win this Test.' He bravely led his side for the second half, passing and tackling with only one arm.

It was a decision which almost certainly saved the series for Britain. The tourists,

43. A despondent Syd Hynes takes the long, lonely walk to the dressing room after becoming the first Rugby League player to be sent off in a Challenge Cup Final at Wembley. Hynes got his marching orders as Leeds crashed to a shock defeat against Leigh in 1971.

given a standing ovation by the partisan Australian crowd, as they returned to the pitch, continued to play brilliant football and they scored three more tries and kicked five goals to win 25–13.

That injury virtually ended Prescott's career. But he could take some comfort in the fact that Britain went on to win the Third Test – and the Ashes.

Even that Third Test produced its share of shocks. More than 68,000 engulfed Sydney Cricket Ground for a match refereed by Queensland's Jack Casey. Britain led 14–12 at the interval and in the second half the game flared up when referee Casey gave Britain a couple of penalties and scrum-half Alex Murphy raced through for a try to the boos and jeers of the crowd.

Australia battled back and winger Moir kicked ahead only to be blatantly obstructed by Ike Southward. Despite this, Moir followed up and almost got the touchdown. But he failed to ground the ball properly and Britain gained possession with winger Mick Sullivan racing the full length of the field for a sensational try.

The crowd went wild and threw bottles, cans, oranges, and apples and everything but the kitchen sink onto the field. No one was hurt and the British players cooled the crowd's temper – one of them caught an orange, calmly peeled it and began to eat, while another picked up an empty bottle and pretended to take a drink. The heat had been taken out of a potentially dangerous situation and Britain coasted to a convincing 40–17 victory.

Steve Llewellyn was one of the great wingers of his time. A Welshman, he played for St Helens and scored some remarkable tries in a glittering career. One touchdown he didn't quite make came in a match against York in the early fifties. Saints were having a field day, scoring at regular intervals. Steve made a blistering break from half-way, cutting through the heart of the Yorkshire defence, and approaching the line found himself quite alone. Nonplussed, he stopped and turned around to check what had gone wrong – a forward pass? Obstruction? Knock-on? Nothing of the sort! The referee was waving play-on, York had simply given up the chase. Unfortunately, Steve hadn't stopped altogether. He was walking – backwards. And he walked over the dead ball line.

On a stormy, rain-swept afternoon in May 1968 Don Fox wrote his name into every book devoted to the story of Rugby League. Don, one of three rugby-playing brothers from the Yorkshire village of Sharlston, had already been awarded the prestigious Lance Todd Trophy as man-of-the-match in the Wembley Cup Final between Leeds and Wakefield Trinity.

Going into the final minute of the match, Trinity were 11–7 down. In that moment Don, who had been on the losing side in five semi-finals with Featherstone, gambled all-or-nothing when he raced to the centre to kick off – following a Bev Risman penalty success for Leeds – instead of scrum-half Ray Owen. He booted the ball into space for winger Ken Hirst who followed up quickly, kicked ahead again and swept in for a touchdown under the sticks.

Fox had pulled off Wembley's most incredible escape act, snatching apparent victory in the final seconds. Trinity were still behind, 11–10, but all that remained was for Fox to kick the easiest of goals from in front of the posts to win by one point.

Such goals Don Fox had been kicking all his rugby career: he scored 503 goals in his years at Featherstone, including a record of twelve in one match, and with Trinity he hit eighty-four goals. Goals such as the last-second shot at Wembley, he could kick with his eyes shut.

There were a few eyes closed, backs turned and heads bowed as Don Fox took extra time and extra care to set up the goal which would take the Challenge Cup to Wakefield for the fifth time. One man sitting in the stands who couldn't bear to watch was Don's brother Neil. A world record goal scorer, Neil was injured and unable to play that day.

In the mud and rain of that 'water-splash' Wembley, Don Fox swung his right boot to hit the goal and claim the glory. He mis-kicked, the ball bobbled wide of the goal and grief-stricken Fox fell to the ground, tears streaming from his eyes. Wakefield had lost the Cup. Bev Risman went to console Fox and as Leeds skipper Mick Clark went to collect the cup the usual scenes of jubilation were subdued.

44. Ray Price, the Australian loose-forward, who scored two tries as the Aussies thrashed Britain in the First Test at Lang Park, Brisbane, in 1979. Also pictured is Wales utility back Bill Francis.

After the game he was awarded the Lance Todd Trophy as the most outstanding player of the 1968 Final. But no one could convince him that he had not won the prize as consolation for missing the kick.

The Challenge Cup Final replay between Halifax and Warrington on 5 May 1954 stands unique in the world of Rugby League. Not for the result, Warrington won 8–4, but for the world record crowd of 102,569 which swamped the Odsal Stadium in Bradford – a stadium situated in a deep channel gouged out of the earth during the Fourth Ice Age 10,000 years ago.

It was a stadium which the then Bradford Northern manager, Harry Hornby, considered not ready to stage such an important match. The lower slopes had been completely terraced with railway sleepers which could be dangerous in bad weather.

68

45. Steve Nash, the Salford and Great Britain scrum-half star, makes a typical break during a first division match against Wigan. Nash was a big match player who saved his best performances for the likes of Australia.

However, in view of the disappointing game at Wembley which had been drawn 4–4, the stadium's capacity was not felt to be at risk.

The kick-off time was changed to 7 p.m. to avoid the rush hour traffic, a shuttle service of fifty buses was running from mid-afternoon and twenty special trains were booked. Thirty-six turnstiles and twenty-four ticket points were in use with more than 100 gatemen and 150 policemen on duty inside and outside the ground.

Although stand tickets were snapped up and fans started queueing four hours before kick-off, the authorities were totally unprepared for the mass invasion which was to follow. More than 60,000 people were inside the ground an hour before the kick-off and police became alarmed as tens of thousands more fans came pouring in. Barriers were forced down and the crowd sat ten deep along the goal lines. Hundreds more climbed onto the roof of the new stand and there were scenes of near panic as spectators fought to get a place and others struggled to escape the crush.

Ambulancemen dealt with more than 200 cases of fainting and the scenes on the roads leading to Odsal resembled an endless flood of refugees. Mile after mile queues of cars, coaches, double-deckers and bikes were stopped in a massive jam as kick-off time approached. Thousands left their vehicles miles from the stadium and walked to Odsal, arriving late in the second half and unable to watch the action. Fans who had travelled by coach gave up hope of seeing the game and listened to it on the vehicle radio while others knocked on the doors of local houses, begging to come in and listen to the commentary.

The official attendance does not take into account the many thousands of gate-crashers who forced their way into the stadium, nor the hordes who were not checked in by harassed gatemen. The chaos didn't stop there. For many fans who had ditched their transport were unable to find their way back and spent the night sleeping in bus shelters and beneath trees.

For the record, Warrington scrum-half Gerry Helme won the Lance Todd Trophy with a dazzling try which clinched the game for the Lancashire side.

There is a stark comparison between the excitement of Odsal's greatest moment and the hollow emptiness of the stadium's lowest gate. That came in 1963 when only 324 spectators watched Northern lose 29–0 to Barrow – the last home match before the original club folded.

Syd Hynes, Leeds' former international centre star, will never forget Saturday 15 May 1971, the day he created Rugby League history. Unfortunately for Syd, he carved his own special place in the record books by becoming the first Rugby League player to be sent off at Wembley. It should have been so different for Hynes. Leeds had made him captain and his side was odds-on favourites to beat unfashionable Leigh and carry off the Challenge Cup.

Everything went wrong for Hynes and Leeds from the start. Leigh, inspired by brilliant player-coach Alex Murphy, opened the score after five minutes and never looked back. The Cup was already lost when, in the sixty-fifth minute, Hynes was involved in a clash with Murphy – who was carried off – and he got his marching orders from Huddersfield referee, Billy Thompson.

Hynes had joined Argentinian soccer star Antonio Rattin as sport's only players to be sent off at the Empire Stadium. Rattin got his marching orders in the World Cup quarter-final match against England in 1966. Worse was to follow for Hynes. Leeds slipped to a humiliating 24–7 defeat and later the Leeds skipper was banned for six matches.

Hynes still believes he shouldn't have been sent off. 'I was supposed to have butted Alex Murphy but I never hit him,' he said later. 'I felt very bitter about the whole business, but that was nothing compared with the shame I felt at being sent off. The long walk to the dressing room seemed never ending and I wished the ground would open up and swallow me. I was the loneliest man in London.'

70

It's perhaps ironic that Lang Park, Brisbane was, at one time, a cemetery. For certainly it was the graveyard for the Ashes-seeking hopes of Great Britain in the summer of 1979. The British squad had already been hit hard by injury as they approached the First Test, but that was little to the trouble they were to find themselves in against the mighty Australians.

Britain were never in the match with a chance. Their dreadful tackling, poor handling, and almost non-existent support-play was in stark contrast to the fast, skilful and physical Australian play. Only packmen George Nicholls, David Ward and Steve Norton gave sound performances, while the cock-a-hoop Kangaroos held all the aces with centre Mick Cronin landing ten goals out of eleven attempts and both winger Kerry Boustead and Ray Price scored two tries apiece as Australia won 35–0.

Little wonder that British coach, Eric Ashton, commented: 'We were terrible. It was humiliating. The Australians were superb in all aspects but our dreadful tackling made it easy for them.'

To make matters worse for Britain, prop Trevor Skerrett was sent off for the first time in his career. Britain never really recovered from that First Test annihilation. The jubilant Australians won the Second and Third Tests to complete their first Test series whitewash in history and to set up a record points total of 87 – beating the previous best in 1963 by four. The Australians had proved themselves worthy of the title of World Champions and it could be a long, long while before anybody knocks them off their throne.

CHAPTER SEVEN

The immortals

Rugby League is a game that breeds courage, a game that breeds dedication and a game that breeds determination. It is also a game that has thrown up more than its share of characters. Players who have not only captivated fans throughout the world with their skill, speed and flair, but who have earned a place in sport's hall of fame. Unfortunately, it just isn't possible to mention them all – that would be a lifetime's work – and so to those we have been forced to omit, we apologise.

Alex Murphy

To many people Alexander J. Murphy is the greatest player ever to lace up rugby boots; to others he is a big head with a mouth to rival that of Muhammed Ali. As both a player and a coach 'Alexander the Great' has generated both admiration and hate from fans and players alike. He has never been far removed from controversy, nor has he been frightened of taking on the establishment.

The irrepressible Murphy has spent his whole Rugby League life courting glory – and the newspaper headlines – but, whatever your opinion of him, he was, and still is, one of the sport's greatest figures.

Murphy has never been slow to sing his own praises. 'I knew when I was twelve years old I was going to be good,' he once said. And after playing in a tour trial match at the tender age of eighteen, he is said to have raced up to the manager and remarked: 'Right, who are the other members of the squad going to Australia with me?'

Fact or fiction, there is no doubt whatsoever that Murphy was one of the game's greatest scrum-halves – if not the greatest. Alex Murphy signed for St Helens as a dazzling, super-gifted 16-year-old in 1955. Two years later he went to Australia with the Great Britain squad as second-choice scrum-half and returned the undisputed king of the No. 7 shirt. Little wonder the Australians still rate him as Britain's best ever scrum-half.

Alex's international career flourished, he won every honour in the game and courted real glory when, at home, he led St Helens to Challenge Cup Final victory over Wigan in 1966.

A long, drawn out dispute at St Helens led to him joining Leigh as coach and he immediately led his team of 'no-hopers' to a Floodlit Trophy Final appearance in 1967 and a 1970 Lancashire Cup Final win. Six months later he brought off his greatest triumph – leading Leigh to a shock Challenge Cup Final triumph over the odds-on favourites Leeds at Wembley.

Then Murphy dropped a real bombshell, he quit Leigh just days later and joined Warrington. Within two years he put the 'Wire' on top of the league and in 1973–4 his side swept to a magnificent four-cup triumph. Warrington's Cup Final triumph over Featherstone Rovers meant that Murphy had become the first player in Rugby League history to skipper three different sides to victory at Wembley.

46. Guess who!

47. That's right – it's the legendary Alexander J. Murphy, here conducting cup operations for Warrington.

His playing career was virtually ended in 1974 when he sustained a jaw injury, but he took Warrington back to Wembley the following year only to sample defeat for the first time. As England coach he only tasted defeat once in eleven games, but he was still replaced as team chief and in August 1978 he moved to Salford. During his playing career Murphy thrilled the crowds with his tremendous natural ability and mastery of the Rugby League skills and, at the same time, he wasn't averse to trying to influence referees.

Naturally he had more than his fair share of enemies – both on and off the field – and on one occasion he was attacked by an angry fan armed with a pair of scissors. After

73

48. Australian international centre star John Cootes breaks for the try-line in a clash against New Zealand at Auckland's Carlaw Park.

49. Father John Cootes celebrates mass during the Australians' World Cup trip to England in 1970. Later Father Cootes was given papal dispensation to marry.

some rather unsavoury incidents in the tunnel after one Warrington match he was heavily fined by the Rugby League and threatened with a total ban from the game. Like him or hate him, Alexander Murphy can never be ignored. His football skills are a great loss to the game, but long may he be a part of Rugby League.

John Cootes

In the rough, tough uncompromising game of Rugby League, Australian Test star John Cootes was just that little bit different. Not that the flattened, broken nose, the stocky, powerful build, or the side-step of a centre star supreme gave anything away – far from it. Like most Rugby League players John Cootes liked to share the odd beer or two and have a laugh and a joke with the rest of his team mates. Yet Cootes was different.

For every Sunday morning he would don vestments and take mass as Father John, a Roman Catholic priest. Father John, from the Blue Mountains of New South Wales, was ordained by Pope Paul VI in 1966 and it was while he was studying theology in Rome that he was spotted playing Rugby Union by an Australian talent scout. Father John went on to play in four Tests against New Zealand and was a star of the 1970 World Championships in England. Yet, even on World Cup match days, he insisted on taking mass and it was rumoured that he once requested a half-time substitution in order to perform a wedding service.

Father John was never upset by the colourful language that is so often heard in rugby changing rooms, nor by some of the unsavoury tactics dished out by opponents. He once said: 'Bad language is all part and parcel of the game and I've heard it all before. Only once have I really gone wild. It happened when a big brute of a forward flattened one of our backs with a diabolical late tackle. Next time he got the ball I went in and tackled him rather hard – mind you, it was all done legally!'

The rugby priest's tour of England was ended by a particularly hard tackle by a Yorkshire forward who, it is said, was upset that he had caused injury to Father John. The forward later wrote a letter of apology to the priest in Australia and some months later he is rumoured to have replied with the words: 'Your apology is accepted, no hard feelings – and should your parents ever care to visit Australia I will be glad to marry them!'

John Cootes didn't earn a penny-piece from playing Rugby League. He was officially listed as an amateur and was paid in 'kind' – surfboards, sporting equipment, and on one occasion, a library for the school where he taught.

Father John also made his mark at sky-diving, skin-diving, tennis, cricket, horse riding, flying aeroplanes, golf, folk singing – in eight languages – snow-skiing and barefoot water skiing.

In 1972 John Cootes left Australia for America and was given Papal dispensation from his priesthood vows to get married.

Christopher Chevasse

Not to be outdone on religious grounds, Britain boasted her own rugby-playing churchman – but around the turn of the century. Christopher Chevasse was an Anglican; starting as a popular curate in St Helens he later became Bishop of Rochester and one of the best-known dignitaries in the Church of England. Reverend Chevasse was chased by several top Rugby Union clubs but opted to play the thirteen-a-side code for St Helens saying: 'Rugby League is the game of my parishioners, so it must be mine also . . . and hang the consequences.' The curate was never again allowed to play Rugby Union – although he never received any payment for playing the game.

St Helens had a reputation in those early days for being a rough side and their spectators, particularly the women, were not averse to using a few choice words of rebuke. On one occasion, a rather well-to-do aristocrat who frowned on the professional game exclaimed: 'Surely you're not playing with that company of sinners?' The curate replied: 'Not sinners, sir – Saints!' Saintly it was. The captain in those days often gave players a dressing-down for swearing during a match 'lest it put the parson off his game'.

The reverend never uttered a foul word or made a dirty tackle in his rugby career, but he was once sent off. After falling asleep while preparing his sermon, he awoke a few minutes before kick-off time. He hurriedly summoned a hansom cab, drew the curtains and changed into his playing gear. Unfortunately, he still arrived late and rushed onto the field – only to be sent off by the referee because a reserve had already taken his place. He was reported for ungentlemanly conduct because he had failed to obtain the referee's permission to go on to the field.

Later, Christopher Chevasse took up the whistle, taking charge of junior games.

50. Mini-maestro Roger Millward meets the Queen Mother before leading Hull KR to their first Challenge Cup triumph in 1980. Looking on is Rovers' chairman Bill Land.

Before games involving teams notorious for roughhouse tactics he would go to the changing rooms and tell players: 'Before sending a player off I always give one warning – this is it!'

Roger Millward

It was on a bleak Saturday at the beginning of October 1980 that the illustrious career of one of Rugby League's greatest players was suddenly brought to a tragic end.

Roger Millward, one of the smallest men to have played the world's toughest game, was making his comeback after leading Hull Kingston Rovers to their first glorious Challenge Cup Final triumph at Wembley the previous May, in a reserve team match against Batley before only a handful of fans at Craven Park. In an off-the-ball tackle Millward was hit about the face and broke his jaw for the fourth time in ten months. He was rushed to hospital, underwent surgery and the following day he turned up to watch his biggest rivals Hull take on New Zealand. With his jaw badly swollen and through clenched teeth, Millward said: 'That's it. I'll not play again.'

76

51. Roger Millward in action for his club Hull Kingston Rovers. Millward, the man the mighty Australians really feared, had his long and illustrious career ended by a broken jaw in October 1980, but not until he had led Rovers to their first Challenge Cup triumph at Wembley the previous May.

Thus ended a glorious professional career which began in October 1963 when he pocketed the princely sum of £200 and signed for his home town club Castleford. Even before then the mini-maestro had captured the hearts of millions of TV viewers when he starred in a series of Sunday morning junior matches.

Millward's brilliance was evident from the start and he played his first international for Britain before he was even a regular in the Castleford team, where he was overshadowed by half-back 'H' Bombs Alan Hardisty and Keith Hepworth.

Castleford found it impossible to keep three great players on their books with only two places at stake. In August 1966 they reluctantly agreed to sell him to Hull Kingston Rovers for a giveaway £6,000. Since that move the Dodger's career really blossomed. He went on to make six trips to Australia and New Zealand with British touring and World Cup teams. He also spent a summer playing for crack Sydney side Cronulla-Sutherland where he was fêted like a film star.

Although Millward is just 5 ft 4 ins tall, he was the one man the all-conquering Australians really feared. They never had anyone to match the skill, flair and all-round brilliance of 'Mighty Mouse'.

Millward played in forty-seven internationals and made twelve county appearances for Yorkshire. But the one representative match he could well have done without was the challenge tie between World Champions Australia and England at Leeds in November 1975. Skippering England for the first time, he had played just eight minutes of football when he was involved in a scuffle with Australia's tigerish scrum-half, Tom Raudonikis, who had been drafted into the side especially to mark him. Millward thrashed around helplessly as Raudonikis piled in with a flurry of punches, and the incident ended with Wakefield referee Fred Lindop sending off both men. It was the first and only time Millward, who is reputed never to have thrown a punch in anger on the field of play, was sent off. After the match he was in tears, and certainly everyone who saw the incident still believes he should never have been given his marching orders.

Millward played 401 senior games for Hull Kingston Rovers, scoring 207 tries, landing 597 goals and 10 drops, an incredible total of 1,825 points. His last appearance brought his finest hour – Rovers' 10–5 Wembley victory over Humberside rivals Hull. Even that occasion was soured by his jaw being broken after only thirteen minutes. Bravely he carried on playing through terrible pain – but, alas, time, age and brutal tactics were fast catching him up. Five months later his playing days were over.

Brian Bevan

The immortal Brian Bevan, with his fragile frame, always looked as if he had walked straight out of a poster for Oxfam. The balding, toothless Bevan, with both knees heavily bandaged, who learned his trade side-stepping around posts in his home city of Sydney, Australia, and Tamarama, came to England as a stoker in the Australian Navy in 1945.

He wanted to play Rugby League for Leeds, but the Headingley club was far from impressed by his lean and hungry look and, disappointed, he crossed the Pennines to play trials with Warrington. After successful trials, he returned home to Australia to be demobbed and later he went back to Warrington to become one of the greatest wingers in the game.

Crowds poured through the turnstiles just to get a glimpse of the man who looked as though a puff of wind would blow him over. Bevan, who once ran 100 yards in 9·9 seconds in soccer gear, was a totally unorthodox player. He could score tries from almost any position – and often did. His most famous try came in the 1948 Charity Cup match against Wigan. Bevan received the ball behind his own line and set off to swerve, side-step and wing his way past all thirteen Wigan players before touching down.

During a career with Warrington and Blackpool which spanned eighteen years up to 1964, Bevan scored 800 tries, twice crossing for seven in a match – against both Leigh and Bramley in 1953. He is the player to come closest to rivalling Huddersfield's Albert Rosenfeld for tries in a season. In 1952–3 he scored seventy-two touchdowns, just eight short of Rosenfeld's magical eighty.

The Athletes

Which player scored in every Rugby League match in which he took part? A popular trick question in pub and club quizzes. The answer – the West Indies' world record sprinter, MacDonald Bailey. He shocked the sporting world when he signed for Leigh in 1953 for a fee of £1,000 – with more to come if he succeeded.

His Leigh team mates put in many hours of extra work to teach the track star the basics of rugby. His debut, in a friendly match against Wigan at Hilton Park, created tremendous interest. Fleet Street writers were out in force, the TV cameras focused on Leigh and the fans packed the terraces. Alas, the Helsinki Olympics bronze medallist, although scoring a touchdown, was out of his depth. His eighty-minute rugby career ended that same night but, at least, Leigh covered the cost of their gamble.

MacDonald's signing did lead to several other athletes – Europe's fastest sprinter Berwyn Jones, Olympic track ace Alf Meakin and shot putt champion Arthur Rowe – trying their hand at the game. Unfortunately, only one, Berwyn Jones, made a success of the new sport.

Under the name of 'Walker', Berwyn Jones played a trial for Wakefield Trinity in March 1964. It was a trial which later shocked the athletics world as Britain prepared for the Tokyo Olympics. The Welshman, who joined Trinity on 31 March, was a member of the British sprint relay team and almost certain to go to Tokyo.

Although there were only a few weeks left of the season, Jones learned a lot and managed to score five tries. The following season he scored twenty-two tries, two of them in matches for Britain against France – the Trinity gamble was paying dividends. In 1966 Berwyn Jones earned himself a place in the British squad to tour Australia and New Zealand, but on his return he lost his first team place and quit the game. He was later persuaded to resume but never recaptured his former glory.

Billy Boston

Billy Boston was the boy wonder of Welsh rugby when two Wigan directors, Joe Taylor and Bill Gore, paid a trip to Cardiff's Tiger Bay. They nervously knocked on his father's door and were given a cool reception. Even so, they were invited into the Boston home and after hours of discussion Billy's father asked them for the then huge fee of £3,000 for his son's signature, convinced that it would put off Rugby League scouts for ever.

It didn't. Wigan agreed and Boston signed professional, making his debut against Barrow in November 1953. He showed such sparkling skills in those early matches that, in less than six months, he was chosen for the 1954 Tour of Australasia. On that tour he scored thirty-six tries and two years later he notched up sixty tries in a season for Wigan – his best year.

52. Rugby League's world record points' scorer Neil Fox.

In his early years Boston relied on speed and skill to beat the opposition. Later, however, he put on extra weight and would power down the wing with speed and strength, swatting would-be tacklers with a flick of the hand.

Boston played a vital part in helping Britain win the Ashes 'Down Under' in 1962 and twice he scored seven tries in a match against Dewsbury in 1955 and Salford in 1962. He

53. Australian tough guy Tom Raudonikis races away from a scrum watched by Rugby League's first Euro-Ref, Ronnie Campbell of Widnes.

represented Great Britain thirty-one times and made three World Cup appearances. During a star-studded career Boston crashed over for more than 500 tries, a try-scoring feat only bettered by the legendary Brian Bevan.

Neil Fox

In April 1979 Neil Fox was officially recognised as the record points scorer of all time. The Rugby League had delayed recognition until a thorough check had been made on the figures of the previous holder, Jim Sullivan. The long and laborious task finally showed that Sullivan had amassed a total of 6,006 points – not including friendly matches which are not recognised for official record purposes – while the brilliant Fox had amassed 6,220 points.

Incredibly, Neil, the son of a former Featherstone Rovers forward and brother of Don and Peter, had broken Sullivan's record on 4 December 1977 without even knowing it. On that day before a crowd of just 753 fans at Doncaster Neil landed three goals and it was the second of those goals that was to create history.

Neil signed for Wakefield Trinity in 1956 where he scored the bulk of his record points total in eighteen years at Belle Vue. At the same time he won three Challenge Cup winner's medals in four years, grabbing a record twenty points haul in the 1960 Final against Hull, and winning the Lance Todd Trophy as man of the match two years later against Huddersfield.

He helped Trinity to their first Championship triumph in 1967 and collected six Yorkshire Cup winner's medals – one with Bradford Northern in 1978. He also appeared in the first John Player Final and won a Premiership medal with Bradford in the same year. His first international cap came in 1959 against Australia and he was a member of the 1962 British Tour squad. He made thirty international appearances and played in every position in club football apart from hooker and open side prop!

Jack Arkwright

Jack, a strong-running second-rower with St Helens and Warrington during the thirties, holds the rare distinction of being sent off twice in the same match. It happened on the 1936 British tour of Australia. The tourists were playing a match against one of the tough provincial teams.

Jack recalls: 'I tackled one of their players a bit hard and another bloke burst up and jumped on me. I thumped him and the referee ordered me off; but their captain, possibly with revenge in mind, made a plea on my behalf. The referee relented.

'After taking more stick and with only two minutes of the match remaining I thumped their captain. The referee spotted me. "All right," I said, "I'm going this time." And I walked.'

Tommy Raudonikis

One of Australia's finest post-war scrum-halves, Tommy Raudonikis, is also a dab-hand at the boxing game, as a sell-out Sydney crowd will verify.

Raudonikis and Australian Test team mate Greg Olliphant, who openly admit to not sending each other Christmas cards, decided to settle their differences in the boxing ring. All tickets for the event were snapped up within two days of going on sale, seconds were appointed, a doctor was on hand and so were the local press to give round by round coverage.

The fight started with both players swinging punches at each other and at the end of the first round they went back to their corners and slumped onto their stools with sweat dripping down their faces.

With the crowd cheering wildly the players came out for the second round. Suddenly, a nasty clash of heads left Olliphant with a jagged gash above an eye. Doctors at the ringside had no hesitation in stopping the bout – despite the protests of Olliphant, who refused to pack it in and nearly hit the officials! Raudonikis just sat there – grinning!

CHAPTER EIGHT

The amateur game

A pie and a pint with the lads, a game of darts, dominoes and snooker. Organ and drums belting out a raucous backing for a busty, blue-eyed blonde who packed biscuits by day and night clubs by night. That was the backcloth to one of the most momentous occasions in the history of sport and the annals of Rugby League.

It was the Day of the Rugby Renaissance. Away from the smoky commotion at the Greenside Working Men's Club in Huddersfield on Sunday 4 March 1973, a group of men met to discuss the ailing game of amateur Rugby League.

Maurice Oldroyd, now the amateur game's Regional Organiser and one of the most influential men in sport, was one of that group. 'We were not men of vision,' he said, 'otherwise we would have held the meeting at the George Hotel where the game of Rugby League was born in 1895. Personally, I wish we had gone to the George, but at least Huddersfield can claim a double birthright.' It was at the Greenside WMC on that cold, Sunday afternoon that the British Amateur Rugby League Association (BARLA) was about to be born.

Ahead of those pioneers was a path as rough and rugged as the Oregon Trail. Within weeks they had been branded as rebels and outlawed by the sport's governing body, the Rugby Football League. The government-backed Sports Council refused to recognise them; they were given the cold shoulder by the Central Council for Physical Recreation and the powerful Universities Athletics Union and they were ostracised by the Rugby Union.

'Nobody liked us!' said Maurice Oldroyd.

But with bloody-minded belligerence, determination and a bank balance of £25 – cash raised from a whip-round at the Greenside WMC – they set about their task of re-organising the amateur game.

Until 1973 the amateurs were under the control of the Rugby League and managed by the council's thirty professional clubs. They had no representation, no voice and no identity. The amateur game was fast losing its respectability. With no control over their own destiny, the amateurs were disorganised, ill-disciplined and were on a chronic trail' of self-destruction. Youth rugby had completely collapsed and many clubs were fading into oblivion.

The birth of BARLA was the re-birth of amateur Rugby League; it channelled new ideas and energies through the pipeline of progress. It began with a fragmented and parochial game, a sprinkling of clubs barely eking out an existence. Yet a few years later Dickie Jeeps, Chairman of the Sports Council and former England Rugby Union star, was to say: 'BARLA has been responsible for one of the most outstanding sporting success stories of the seventies – the remarkable growth of Rugby League Football.'

Ironically, the 'BARLA' tag happened by accident. Maurice Oldroyd explained, 'We originally called ourselves the British Amateur Rugby League Committee – BARLC.

54. St Helens Recs pictured in 1933. They never re-appeared after the Second World War.

Then the solicitor who was handling our affairs happened to say: "I suppose you'll be calling yourself BARLA for short." So we did.'

BARLA moved from strength to strength, producing the game's first ever National Five Year Development Plan, the blueprint for the successful years to follow. Youth rugby developed rapidly and in 1977 there was a trail-blazing tour of Australia and New Zealand; in 1980 the Australian Combined High Schools paid a return visit, playing a Test Match at Headingley.

The amateurs also conquered the universities. Almost all Northern universities now have a Rugby League side and teams have been established at Swansea, Oxford and Cambridge. The sport is now recognised by the Universities Athletic Union.

But perhaps BARLA's most memorable feat was the historic 1978 tour of Papua New Guinea, Australia and New Zealand. The tour of Papua was not only the first full Rugby League tour of that country but also the first major tour by any sporting body in the world. Papua reciprocated that visit in 1979 with matches at St Helens, in Cumbria and on Humberside.

Yet the BARLA pioneers must have felt they were banging their heads against a brick wall back in 1973 when, tremulously, they approached the Rugby League to ask for a meeting. No! BARLA was rebuffed, strong sanctions were imposed and all financial assistance to the amateurs was withdrawn.

Curiously, it was the very fact that BARLA consisted entirely of enthusiastic amateurs willing to give every moment of spare time in their fight for the amateur cause, which was the strength and the weapon which won the war of the angry silence. Within twelve months hostilities had ended, total opposition had become unanimous support and towards the end of 1974 BARLA officials Maurice Oldroyd, Bob Beal and Tom Keaveney journeyed to London with Rugby League bosses Brian Snape (chairman)

84

and David Oxley (secretary) to meet the Sports Council's Roger Bannister. It was Rugby League abdication day.

Maurice Oldroyd recalls: 'My heart was in my mouth. It was the most momentous occasion in my rugby life. We sat around the table, discussing the future of the game, professionalism, the amateurs. Then came the question to Brian Snape from Roger Bannister: "Do you mean you wish to abdicate ALL responsibility for the amateur game?"

'My mouth was dry, and my palms were wet. The room was still and yet it was spinning around in my mind. This was it! This was what it was all about! This was the real beginning of BARLA. It was now or never.

'The reply seemed to take an eternity, but Salford chairman, Mr Snape, his face without expression, simply said: "Yes."

'In that moment the British Amateur Rugby League Association took over full responsibility for the running of the amateur game; we were officially recognised as the sport's governing body.'

BARLA, with its unimpeachable amateur status, was then in a position to qualify for grant aid – provided the association could be shown to be financially sound. Funds were desperately needed and it was decided every player registered with an amateur club should pay £1 per season to BARLA. A year later they did indeed qualify for their first grant; they were on a sound footing and progress had been exciting and spectacular. Hundreds of cup games had been organised and played, plus regional matches and international fixtures.

The year 1976 saw progress off the field, too, with Maurice Oldroyd appointed as full-time Regional Organiser and BARLA – through Sports Council aid – opening its own headquarters in Huddersfield, the opening ceremony performed by Minister of Sport Denis Howell.

BARLA boasts that through its development work one new club or team is born every week of the season. Progress has been such that the 1973 figure of 170 clubs in 25 leagues (one team per club) now reads in excess of 340 clubs, 850 teams and 30 leagues, with thousands more players attracted to the game at all levels.

Much toil and effort has been channelled into youth rugby, the life blood of any sport, and here BARLA have scored a magnificent triumph in quantity and quality. Youth rugby has increased more than ten-fold and two former Great Britain captains, Barry Banks (Hull) and Steve Evans (Featherstone), have already made international appearances as professionals. Leeds' half-back Kevin Dick, another BARLA starlet, thrilled a world-wide TV audience with his brilliance in the 1977 Challenge Cup Final at Wembley, and won a unanimous vote from the Rugby League Writers' Association to take the prestigious Harry Sunderland Trophy as man of the match in the Premiership Final of 1979.

It is at school where youngsters receive their first taste of competitive Rugby League through the English Schools' Rugby League. It is under-11 sides – the Mini Marvels – who compete in one of the BARLA showpiece matches of the season: the curtain-raiser before the Wembley Cup Final, watched by 95,000 fans in the stadium and millions through the medium of television.

Schoolboy and youth Rugby League has been established in Scotland, at Hamilton and Edinburgh, and this has been supported by the London Schools and Youth League.

At under-16 level there is the prospect of regular international matches against

55. 'The Kumuls are coming!' Two of the Papua New Guinea tourists to France and Britain pictured in national costume.

France – but it was at under-18 level that, in 1977, the year of the Queen's Silver Jubilee, BARLA and youth rugby were given great boosts with a pioneering tour of the Antipodes. The Sports Council backed the trip with a substantial grant, the balance being raised by the players and by public appeal. A party of twenty players made the trip led by tour managers Douglas Hird and Alan Lancaster.

86

From Manchester they went via Los Angeles, Honolulu and Fiji to New Zealand where they played two matches; the second against a New Zealand XIII at Christchurch being a curtain-raiser to the New Zealand–Great Britain World Cup match.

The boys played three matches in Australia, the last one against an Australian XIII preceded the World Cup Final between Australia and Great Britain. That youth clash (won 21–13 by the Australian youngsters) was filmed for BARLA and is now used for development projects, being shown throughout the country.

Universities Rugby League dates back to 1967 when Andrew Cudbertson, with several students in the chemistry faculty at Leeds University, decided it was time to add the sport of Rugby League to the college's curriculum. One of the first problems facing the enthusiasts was one of opposition – who to play! Andrew finally found opponents at the University of Liverpool and that historic colleges clash took place at Widnes with Leeds running out winners 32–16.

Rugby League interest in the Universities began to increase and by 1968 clubs had been formed at Bradford, Salford and Manchester. When Sheffield joined the Rugby League ranks a year later it was the signal for the start of the Universities League, numbers having also been swelled by clubs from Hull, Lancaster and Nottingham Universities. Later came a second period of expansion with clubs from Leeds Polytechnic, Loughborough College of Art, Huddersfield Polytechnic, Manchester Polytechnic and the Universities of Reading and Surrey joining the league.

With the league operating so well it was inevitable that internationals would follow. The first was played at Salford in April 1973 when English Universities met French Universities, now a regular fixture on the colleges' calendar. France won that first match 17–11, and England were captained by half-back John Roberts of Sheffield, who was later to go down in history as the first player from the Universities League to go on tour. He was in the 1978 party in the BARLA Pacific Tour of Papua New Guinea, Australia and New Zealand.

The Universities have perhaps been foremost in taking the game outside the accepted Northern boundaries of Rugby League. Peter Tate, a postgraduate involved in the birth of the game at Sheffield, set up a club at Portsmouth Polytechnic. There are also clubs at Swansea, in the heart of the Welsh Rugby Union stronghold, and at Oxford.

All this despite antiquated opposition from the Rugby Union authorities. The Rugby Union impose a life ban on any player 'should they play, coach or have any connection whatsoever with the sport of Amateur Rugby League Football'. Such a ruling belongs to the era of witch-hunting and superstition of seventeenth-century England; it is anti-sport; it is hideous apartheid practised by a body of fuddy-duddies for whom the true meaning of sporting integrity and brotherhood has been lost in the cobwebs of time.

Nearly a century has passed since the 'original sin' of 1895, when the Northern clubs committed their mortal misdemeanour in the breakaway from the Rugby Union in the row over broken time payments. But the words 'forgive and forget' do not come within the vocabulary of the Rugby Union hierarchy. Still they shun the thirteen-a-side game, still they penalise the sportsmen who love rugby (Union and League) and would like the chance to play both openly.

Instances of discrimination against fellow sportsmen are, sadly, commonplace. There was the incredible case of a convicted murderer who, serving a life sentence, joined the prison's Rugby Union team. But the RFU discovered he had once played Rugby League – and banned him.

56. George Fairbairn, the Wigan player-coach who is a Scotsman, but has played for England and captained Great Britain. Man of Steel in 1980.

Another target for Rugby Union hypocrisy was a 1977 representative match involving English Universities and the Southern League. Plans for the historic match had been laid well in advance and the game was to be played at Oxford Old Boys' RUFC, a ground belonging to the local Education Authority, while the clubhouse was the property of the club. All was going well – there was even a tour match arranged against Oxford University represented by Corpus Christi College (and a sprinkling of southern stars).

Then, totally out of the blue, came a warning to Union players planning to play Rugby League – even at amateur level. The Oxford Old Boys' Club, fearing reprisals, withdrew their offer of facilities on instructions from Oxfordshire County RFU. All was not totally lost. The East Midlands Bus Company offered the use of their social club for the reception and the match was played on a nearby park pitch.

Incredibly, the RFU had their last insane laugh with another act of sporting skulduggery. One of the stars of the Southern team was prop-forward Bob Mahuta, a Maori from Auckland and a graduate in anthropology. Keep-fit fanatic Bob played Union on Saturdays and Amateur Rugby League on the Sabbath. Shortly after his spot of exercise in the front row for the Southern side against the Universities, he was barred from ever playing Union again. His subscriptions were returned to him. Or, in other words, because Bob would not play by their silly rules, the RFU took their ball home.

The Rugby Football Union is justly proud of its true blue traditions of amateurism. Yet few touring teams from the fifteen-a-side code can surely match the amateur status of BARLA's historic 1978 tour of the South Pacific. It lasted thirty-eight days, covered over 30,000 miles, involving nine vigorous games in Papua New Guinea, New Zealand and Australia.

The players who went not only lost six weeks wages, but had to buy their own blazers and trousers and provide their own spending money. BARLA did not even re-imburse out-of-pocket expenses. There was an ironic cheer when, at the final training session at Carnegie College in Leeds, it was announced that each player would receive an official tie – free of charge!

Thirty-six hours after leaving London the party of thirty-two, including twenty-six players, were met at Port Moresby, the Papuan capital, by British High Commissioner Donald Middleton and Dr Jim Jacobi, president of the Papua New Guinea Rugby Football League.

The first match was to be played at Rabaul where the temperature sizzled in the high nineties and the humidity made it difficult to breathe. The tourists had a training session within hours of arrival and were astonished to see a crowd of 800 locals waiting to watch them, many climbing the tall coconut trees which surrounded the ground to get a better vantage point.

The game itself was watched by a capacity crowd of 5,600 which jammed into the Queen's Park ground, and thousands more were locked out. Britain won a convincing 41–13 victory. Then came the infamous 'Charge of the Lae Brigade' match against Northern Zone. More than 5,500 locals crammed into the stadium for the floodlit game. It was a match punctuated by penalties and scrums and devoid of attacking football. The locals became increasingly restless and in the final minutes they became inflamed by the heated exchanges on the field which saw two Britons sent off. It all began in the seventy-second minute when British winger Steve Critchenson was given his marching orders

57. Kevin Dick, Leeds' brilliant scrum-half.

after being involved in a flare-up. Two minutes later second rower Ronnie Carter was alleged to have thrown a punch at a Northern Zone player and was also sent off.

Suddenly, 400 locals charged across the field and several British players were sent hurtling to the ground as they struggled to reach the safety of the dressing rooms under the main grandstand. British centre Dennis Oaten, who disappeared under a mass of angry fans, was so badly hurt that he didn't play again on the tour. Oaten, who was rescued by Papuan players, suffered eye, knee and ankle injuries, while scrum-half Jimmy Green, loose-forward Paul Dowling and substitute John Eastwood were all injured by the marauders.

After ninety minutes of terror in the dressing room, which had heavily barred windows, they were saved by the arrival of baton-waving riot police who, with their dogs, escorted the tourists back to the safety of their Lae headquarters – the local army barracks!

The game was declared 'no result' although Northern Zone were leading 4–2 when the trouble erupted.

These disgraceful scenes almost brought the historic tour to a sudden halt. However, after many hours of deliberation the tour party decided to continue and at Mount Hagen they received a rapturous welcome from the Highlands tribespeople. Britain won a thrilling match 26–25 and then, before a crowd of 9,000, they were beaten 27–15 by Southern Zone. The stage was set for a fitting finale to the tour – a Test match at Port Moresby. The tourists shocked the local pundits, who were convinced that Papua would win, by turning on a magnificent display of football to run out 28–7 victors before a capacity crowd of 14,100, with Critchenson striding in for a hat-trick of tries.

The British team for that first Test against Papua New Guinea was: Peter Glover, Jimmy Power, John McCabe, John Roberts, Steve Critchenson, Peter Moore, Jimmy Green, Dave Dykes, Dave Robinson, Ronnie Carter, Alan Varty, Rod Lewis, Paul Dowling (captain). Substitutes: Joey Hull, Jeff Catling, Ernie Lowe and Roger Blair.

Two matches in Australia attracted the smallest crowds of the tour. Both games were played in Sydney – the heart of Australian Rugby League land. The first, at Balmain, was against Combined Universities and was played under floodlights. The students, watched by 1,850, won 28–2, but at Macquarie University, against another student side, the Britons gained revenge, winning 23–10.

Then came a couple of matches in New Zealand where the tourists were beaten 20–13 by Wellington, but went on to beat Waikato 7–5 in a match televised live for the New Zealand TV Service.

The Kumuls, the colourful tourists from Papua New Guinea, made their first trip to Europe in 1979, playing matches in both France and Britain.

Out went the cry, 'The Kumuls are coming.' Although the Papuans played attractive football with their textbook tackling and colourful skills in attack, they never really hit top form. There can be little doubt, though, that within the next few years the Papuans, with their exotic Bird of Paradise emblem, will become a force in World Rugby League.

Away from the paradise of Papua, isolated pockets of amateur Rugby League have sprung up throughout Britain. None perhaps more curious than the development of the game in Scotland. Salford man Henry Callaghan took the game north of the Border when he took up the challenge to teach the sport at his son's school in Hamilton. In September 1976 the first competitive game of Rugby League was played in Scotland between two school sides, St Mary's and St John's. Soon afterwards Hamilton Lions ARLFC was launched and later, following discussions with BARLA, the Scottish Amateur Rugby League Association was formed.

In the next season British national coaches Albert Fearnley and Laurie Gant went to Scotland to assist in coaching. Only one Scot, Wigan's international full-back George Fairbairn, the 1980 Man of Steel, is currently rated among the game's top professionals. The development of Rugby League in Scotland at grass roots level will ensure the figure doesn't remain at one for much longer.

The sport at all amateur levels is booming with hundreds of clubs now running several teams for all age groups. Particular emphasis is being placed on the development of clubhouse facilities.

Through the amateur ranks the game has been re-established in traditional Rugby League areas including Barnsley, Elland and two of the game's 1895 pioneers, Brighouse and Runcorn. The status of the amateur game continues to grow in every respect and this was reflected in 1977 when the Association secretary, Tom Keaveney, was awarded the MBE in the Queen's Birthday Honours List. This was a well-deserved tribute to a remarkable man, who despite suffering from muscular dystrophy, travels 20,000 miles each season to spread the gospel.

The aim of BARLA is simply to spread the amateur game throughout the British Isles and they hope to become a national sport by 1995 – a hundred years after the birth of Rugby League.

At the close of 1980 a crack appeared in the Rugby Union's icy stand towards the thirteen-a-side code when the English Union finally acknowledged BARLA as an official governing body. They also recommended that amateur League players could, if they wished, revert to playing Rugby Union. But they refused a 'free gangway' between the codes by insisting that no player could simultaneously be a playing member of both a League and a Union club.

BARLA chiefs were delighted at the move but frustrated and disappointed that Twickenham had not seen fit to break down finally and completely the barriers dividing the handling code. National Administrator Maurice Oldroyd said: 'We are fighting for the pride and honour of Rugby League. Why should young people wishing to play our sport be intimidated and treated like second-class citizens? It is a wholly unacceptable affront to personal liberties.

'BARLA is striving to make Rugby League a truly national sport, but the excellent pioneer work of our members, particularly those of the Southern and University Leagues, is constantly harassed and hindered by archaic Union dogma which prevents people from playing or even associating with our sport.

'Surely the genuine amateur rugby player of either code should be entitled to the same rights and dignity as every other sportsman in the country. After all, the Rugby Union willingly allow their members to play as professionals in every other sport. Why then should they prevent them from playing Amateur Rugby League?'

CHAPTER NINE

What next?

Rugby League, the game that has had to face so many battles simply to survive, stands on the threshold of a glorious future.

Long gone are the days when merely to exist was a major triumph and long gone are the prophets of doom, who would have liked nothing better than to hammer the final nail into Rugby League's coffin. The game, that once faced the brunt of many a music hall joke and was ridiculed by people who didn't know a goal-keeper from a scrum-half, had made even the experts sit up and take note.

Rugby League is not only here to stay, as it has been for nearly ninety years, but it is quite ready to break out of its four county confines of Lancashire, Yorkshire, Cumbria and, since the local government re-organisation, Cheshire.

It was on 27 June 1980 that Fulham made history by becoming the first soccer outfit to join the professional Rugby League game. The London soccer club, faced with failing finances and a slump in attendances, turned to Rugby League in a bid to cut their over-heads. After lengthy talks between League chiefs Jack Myerscough, David Oxley and David Howes and Fulham chairman Ernie Clay and financial director Brian Dalton, the soccer club's application to join the Second Division of the Rugby League was made.

The application came up before the Rugby League's annual meeting at the Majestic Hotel, Harrogate, a meeting attended by representatives from twenty-nine of the thirty professional clubs. Only Huyton was missing. Fulham chairman Ernie Clay addressed the meeting and, after answering several questions, the vote was taken. Twenty-six clubs came out in favour of their entry into the Rugby League and three others abstained – Fulham were on their way.

The London club made their first signing on 1 July, persuading Cup giants Widnes to part with their skipper Reg Bowden for a £20,000 fee. Bowden, who led the Naughton Park side to every honour in the game during his last five years with them, joined Fulham as player-coach. During the next ten weeks Bowden and director Harold Genders built up a squad of seventeen players at a cost of nearly £150,000, and on 14 September Fulham stepped out for the first Rugby League game against Wigan.

More than 9,500 fans – double the crowds that turned up to watch the soccer side in action – packed into Fulham's Craven Cottage ground and they were treated to a feast of Rugby League football as the home side slammed Wigan, one of the game's greatest names, 24–5. In the space of just eighty minutes ardent soccer fans had turned to Rugby League and, what was just as important, officials from many more soccer clubs were on hand to see the Fulham venture get off the ground and liked what they saw. Crystal Palace, Bolton Wanderers, Charlton Athletic and Luton Town were among a host of soccer clubs that showed more than a passing interest in fielding Rugby League teams.

It was the dawning of a new era. London fans had been given the opportunity of watching Rugby League live and on a regular basis for the first time since the days of Streatham and Acton in the late thirties. It would seem only commonsense that soccer

58. Birth of a rugby club. Fulham, the RL team based on a famous soccer club, play their first match against Wigan in September 1980.

clubs, who are losing thousands of pounds a week, should make full use of their amenities. Both soccer and Rugby League are professional sports. They can not only live side by side amicably but go on to help each other thrive.

Rugby League has found a new image – an image based on vitality and, incredibly, prosperity. While major professional sports, like soccer, face a recession that is biting deep, Rugby League is flourishing. Obviously there will never be a return to the glory days of the forties and the fifties, but Rugby League is doing far more than just surviving.

Attendances hit rock bottom in the early 1970s when the game lost more than half a million fans in just four seasons. Season after season Rugby League headquarters in Leeds lurched despairingly from one set of crisis talks to another and there looked to be no end to the despair. Then new League Secretary David Oxley and Public Relations Officer David Howes brought a fresh approach to the game. They weren't miracle workers but they realised that they had to lift the morale of Rugby League, brighten up its image and to go out and sell the game. As David Oxley so rightly said: 'There were a lot of good people in Rugby League, but morale was so low, they needed to be given a boost – they needed to believe in Rugby League again.'

David Howes set about improving the game's image. A new Rugby League symbol was designed and a more professional approach to the game was adopted. They both realised that the sport could not survive through the turnstiles alone and that sponsorship should play an increasing part in the game's financial survival.

Immediately the fresh, new approach brought an increase through the turnstiles and in 1977 attendances topped the magical million mark for the first time in more than a decade. At the end of the 1979–80 season gates were up for the fourth time in five years, while Football League attendances dropped by five million in four years.

Rugby League was swinging along to the slogan of 'A man's game for all the family'. Part of the increase could well be put down to disillusioned soccer fans – fans repulsed

94

59. Soccer great Malcolm Macdonald, the former Arsenal and England World Cup striker and Fulham RL director, meets Wigan greats Ernie Ashcroft, Billy Boston, Mick Sullivan, Billy Blan, Gordon Ratcliffe, Johnny Lawrenson, Joe Egan and Jim Parr.

60. Fulham player-coach Reg Bowden in action for Widnes against Leeds in the 1977 Challenge Cup Final.

61. Tough training for Warrington. Former British RU Lion and British RL tourist John Bevan leads team mates at a stiff strength-sapping training session on 'The Hill' – the sand dunes at Southport.

by the ever increasing acts of violence that week after week mar the game. Generally, Rugby League is free from such atrocities and fans know that they don't have to go to matches fearing for their own and their family's safety. At the same time the game and top officials are well aware that the comparatively small group of professional yobbos who follow soccer could switch to Rugby League. It is to be hoped that this band of hooligans keeps well away from the thirteen-a-side game – it just doesn't need them.

In the mid-seventies revenue from sponsorship was a mere £20,000 – now it tops the £200,000 mark and every competition in the game has a backer. Sponsorship hasn't been without its critics, but as David Howes points out: 'When you enter the world of sponsorship you do sacrifice some of your freedom as administrators, but Rugby League is just not in the position of being self-supporting through the gates.

96

'Rugby League has a direct commitment to sponsorship, but at the same time any final decisions will always be made by the League.'

Sponsorship is here to stay and, with the advent of the game in London, there could be even more rich pickings for the clubs and League alike. Although the game is spreading in England, attendances are on the increase, and sponsorship is providing an ever-increasing sum of much needed cash, not everything in the Rugby League garden is rosy.

Even allowing for the introduction of sponsorship, in Australia interest in the game is waning. Crowds are falling each year and only the top games attract the big crowds of twenty thousand plus. At the same time crowd control has become a problem over the last few years, especially at the Cumberland Oval, the home of Parramatta. Fencing and barbed wire has been introduced to protect players and referees from the rather partisan crowd that has grown up in the Western Suburbs of Sydney. In 1980 Canterbury suffered the same fate after a clash between Canterbury and Wests erupted into a brawl with spectators jumping the fence to join in.

Luckily for the game those sort of scenes haven't repeated themselves, but anger amongst the crowds is growing. It is to be hoped that throughout the entire Rugby League playing world the future leads to an increase in clubs, an increase in crowds and a decrease in violence.

At the same time would it be too much to ask that those patrons of the ridiculous – the Rugby Football Union – see sense and drop the stupid apartheid they practise against anyone connected with Rugby League. In our present so-called forward-thinking society it is amazing that the Union authorities are allowed to get away with threatening their players, their officials and their referees with a life ban from their game of Rugby Union if they have anything to do with Rugby League. Not only is that life ban archaic, but it is against the true spirit of life itself. Can anybody tell us why a Rugby Union player should be allowed to play professional soccer, professional cricket and professional golf, but not Amateur Rugby League?

Rugby League players are not riddled with some contagious disease. They are just human beings and, as such, should be treated like them. The Rugby Union have absolutely nothing to fear from the League game. If top players from the fifteen-a-side game want to get paid for getting knocked about week after week, then nothing the Rugby Union can do will stop them. It is purely the choice of the individual.

It is to be hoped that the future of Rugby League leads to closer co-operation with the Union game. At least then the scores of Union players who turn out for League sides will not have to hide; and neither will the scores of League players who turn out for Union sides. It would also put an end to the embarrassing situation one player found himself in not so long ago. After finishing with Rugby League because of injury this one player decided to take up Rugby Union and did so well that he was called up to play for Lancashire – unfortunately, discretion was the better part of valour and he withdrew.

Rugby League and Rugby Union have so much to offer each other and all the Union is doing is cutting off its nose to spite its face. The brilliant David Watkins, an International at both the Union and League games, wanted to put something back into the game which first gave him a start – Rugby Union. Sadly the Welsh authorities wouldn't allow him to coach schoolboys in the skills of Rugby Union, because he had played as a professional. How ridiculous can anybody be?

The sooner both codes get together the better it will be for everybody. Only then will it be possible to put an end to the age old argument about who would finish on top if a League side played a Union team.

Sport – pastime; good fellow; honest; straightforward person; broadminded person; good loser; one willing to take a chance; fair-mindedness; generosity towards opponent.

Sport should unite the world. It should know no barriers. It should not be imprisoned by politics, race, colour or creed. Yet sport has been tainted by oppression, hate and political bloody-mindedness – in South Africa, in China, by the Olympic boycott by the African countries in 1976 and the Western boycott of the 1980 Moscow Games because of the invasion of Afghanistan by Russia.

Rugby has been the subject of the longest feud in the history of sport. Barriers created in 1895 are still hard to breach now nearly ninety years on. Now, in these enlightened times, surely Rugby Union and Rugby League can come together, differences forgotten, hatchets buried – Rugby United.

We issue a challenge to the two codes. Break the barriers, come to a sensible settlement and seal it with a match, Rugby Union versus Rugby League. It happened during the war, now let it happen again during peace.

United – in the true tradition of sport.

Appendix

The Challenge Cup

Launched in 1897, it is Rugby League's most prestigious trophy. The Final has been staged at Wembley since 1929 and is the game's showpiece event of every season, screened live to millions on television and watched by a capacity crowd at the Empire Stadium.

Most people remember the Cup Finalists. Here, we present a unique record showing the Cup winners and runners-up plus the beaten semi-finalists.

The first column shows the Cup winners, the second the team they beat in the semi-final; the next column shows the Cup runners-up and the final column the team they beat in the semi-final.

1897	BATLEY	Warrington	ST HELENS	Swinton
1898	BATLEY	Salford	BRADFORD	Widnes
1899	OLDHAM	Leigh	HUNSLET	Salford
1900	SWINTON	Leeds Parish Church	SALFORD	Widnes
1901	BATLEY	Oldham	WARRINGTON	Castleford
1902	BROUGHTON RANGERS	Hunslet	SALFORD	Batley
1903	HALIFAX	Hull	SALFORD	Oldham
1904	HALIFAX	Hunslet	WARRINGTON	Bradford
1905	WARRINGTON	Bradford	HULL KR	Broughton Rangers
1906	BRADFORD	Batley	SALFORD	Keighley
1907	WARRINGTON	Swinton	OLDHAM	Salford
1908	HUNSLET	Broughton Rangers	HULL	Leigh
1909	WAKEFIELD	Wigan	HULL	Halifax
1910	LEEDS	Warrington	HULL	Salford
1911	BROUGHTON RANGERS	Rochdale	WIGAN	Batley
1912	DEWSBURY	Halifax	OLDHAM	Wakefield
1913	HUDDERSFIELD	Wakefield	WARRINGTON	Dewsbury
1914	HULL	Huddersfield	WAKEFIELD	Broughton Rangers
1915	HUDDERSFIELD	Wigan	ST HELENS	Rochdale
1920	HUDDERSFIELD	Oldham	WIGAN	Hull
1921	LEIGH	Rochdale	HALIFAX	Huddersfield
1922	ROCHDALE	Widnes	HULL	Wigan
1923	LEEDS	Barrow	HULL	Wigan
1924	WIGAN	Barrow	OLDHAM	Huddersfield
1925	OLDHAM	Rochdale	HULL KR	Leeds
1926	SWINTON	Hull	OLDHAM	Wigan Highfield
1927	OLDHAM	Wakefield	SWINTON	Dewsbury
1928	SWINTON	Hull	WARRINGTON	Leeds

1929	WIGAN	St Helens Recs	DEWSBURY	Castleford
1930	WIDNES	Barrow	ST HELENS	Wigan
1931	HALIFAX	St Helens	YORK	Warrington
1932	LEEDS	Halifax	SWINTON	Wakefield
1933	HUDDERSFIELD	Leeds	WARRINGTON	St Helens
1934	HUNSLET	Huddersfield	WIDNES	Oldham
1935	CASTLEFORD	Barrow	HUDDERSFIELD	Hull
1936	LEEDS	Huddersfield	WARRINGTON	Salford
1937	WIDNES	Wigan	KEIGHLEY	Wakefield
1938	SALFORD	Swinton	BARROW	Halifax
1939	HALIFAX	Leeds	SALFORD	Wigan

Second World War. A war-time competition was introduced. Not every team was able to compete.

1941	LEEDS	Bradford	HALIFAX	Wakefield
1942	LEEDS	Oldham	HALIFAX	Wigan
1943	DEWSBURY	Oldham	LEEDS	Keighley
1944	BRADFORD	Halifax	WIGAN	Leeds
1945	HUDDERSFIELD	Halifax	BRADFORD	Keighley

Peace-time competition resumed at the start of the 1945–6 season.

1946	WAKEFIELD	Hunslet	WIGAN	Widnes
1947	BRADFORD	Warrington	LEEDS	Wakefield
1948	WIGAN	Rochdale	BRADFORD	Hunslet
1949	BRADFORD	Barrow	HALIFAX	Huddersfield
1950	WARRINGTON	Leeds	WIDNES	Bradford
1951	WIGAN	Warrington	BARROW	Leeds
1952	WORKINGTON	Barrow	FEATHERSTONE	Leigh
1953	HUDDERSFIELD	Wigan	ST HELENS	Warrington
1954	WARRINGTON	Leeds	HALIFAX	Hunslet
1955	BARROW	Hunslet	WORKINGTON	Featherstone
1956	ST HELENS	Barrow	HALIFAX	Wigan
1957	LEEDS	Whitehaven	BARROW	Leigh
1958	WIGAN	Rochdale	WORKINGTON	Featherstone
1959	WIGAN	Leigh	HULL	Featherstone
1960	WAKEFIELD	Featherstone	HULL	Oldham
1961	ST HELENS	Hull	WIGAN	Halifax
1962	WAKEFIELD	Featherstone	HUDDERSFIELD	Hull KR
1963	WAKEFIELD	Warrington	WIGAN	Hull KR
1964	WIDNES	Castleford	HULL KR	Oldham
1965	WIGAN	Swinton	HUNSLET	Wakefield
1966	ST HELENS	Dewsbury	WIGAN	Leeds
1967	FEATHERSTONE	Leeds	BARROW	Dewsbury
1968	LEEDS	Wigan	WAKEFIELD	Huddersfield
1969	CASTLEFORD	Wakefield	SALFORD	Warrington
1970	CASTLEFORD	St Helens	WIGAN	Hull KR
1971	LEIGH	Huddersfield	LEEDS	Castleford
1972	ST HELENS	Warrington	LEEDS	Halifax

100

1973	FEATHERSTONE	Castleford	BRADFORD	Dewsbury
1974	WARRINGTON	Dewsbury	FEATHERSTONE	Leigh
1975	WIDNES	Wakefield	WARRINGTON	Leeds
1976	ST HELENS	Keighley	WIDNES	Featherstone
1977	LEEDS	St Helens	WIDNES	Hull KR
1978	LEEDS	Featherstone	ST HELENS	Warrington
1979	WIDNES	Bradford	WAKEFIELD	St Helens
1980	HULL KR	Halifax	HULL	Widnes

Challenge Cup winners:

- 10 Leeds
- 7 Wigan
- 6 Huddersfield
- 5 St Helens, Wakefield, Warrington, Widnes
- 4 Bradford, Halifax
- 3 Batley, Castleford, Oldham, Swinton
- 2 Broughton Rangers, Dewsbury, Featherstone, Hunslet, Leigh
- 1 Barrow, Hull, Hull KR, Rochdale, Salford, Workington

Most finals:

- 15 Wigan
- 14 Leeds
- 12 Warrington
- 10 Halifax, St Helens
- 9 Hull, Widnes
- 8 Bradford, Huddersfield, Wakefield
- 7 Oldham, Salford

Lance Todd Trophy winners for the outstanding player of the Challenge Cup Final at Wembley – voted by members of the Rugby League Writers' Association:

1946	Billy Stott	Wakefield Trinity
1947	Willie Davies	Bradford Northern
1948	Frank Whitcombe	Bradford Northern
1949	Ernest Ward	Bradford Northern
1950	Gerry Helme	Warrington
1951	Ces Mountford	Wigan
1952	Billy Iveson	Workington Town
1953	Peter Ramsden	Huddersfield
1954	Gerry Helme	Warrington
1955	Jack Grundy	Barrow
1956	Alan Prescott	St Helens
1957	Jeff Stevenson	Leeds
1958	Rees Thomas	Wigan
1959	Brian McTigue	Wigan
1960	Tommy Harris	Hull
1961	Dick Huddart	St Helens
1962	Neil Fox	Wakefield Trinity

1963	Harold Poynton	Wakefield Trinity
1964	Frank Collier	Widnes
1965	Brian Gabbitas	Hunslet } (The award was shared)
	Ray Ashby	Wigan
1966	Len Killeen	St Helens
1967	Carl Dooler	Featherstone Rovers
1968	Don Fox	Wakefield Trinity
1969	Malcolm Reilly	Castleford
1970	Bill Kirkbride	Castleford
1971	Alex Murphy	Leigh
1972	Kel Coslett	St Helens
1973	Steve Nash	Featherstone Rovers
1974	Derek Whitehead	Warrington
1975	Ray Dutton	Widnes
1976	Geoff Pimblett	St Helens
1977	Steve Pitchford	Leeds
1978	George Nicholls	St Helens
1979	David Topliss	Wakefield Trinity
1980	Brian Lockwood	Hull Kingston Rovers

Tries in a Season

80	Albert Rosenfeld	Huddersfield	1913–14
78	Albert Rosenfeld	Huddersfield	1911–12
72	Brian Bevan	Warrington	1952–53
71	Lionel Cooper	Huddersfield	1951–52
68	Brian Bevan	Warrington	1950–51
67	Brian Bevan	Warrington	1953–54
66	Lionel Cooper	Huddersfield	1954–55
65	Lionel Cooper	Huddersfield	1948–49
63	Johnny Ring	Wigan	1925–26
63	Brian Bevan	Warrington	1954–55
60	Billy Boston	Wigan	1956–57
58	Eric Harris	Leeds	1930–31
57	Brian Bevan	Warrington	1947–48
57	Brian Bevan	Warrington	1955–56
56	Albert Rosenfeld	Huddersfield	1912–13
56	Albert Rosenfeld	Huddersfield	1914–15
56	Brian Bevan	Warrington	1948–49
55	Stanley Moorhouse	Huddersfield	1911–12
55	Alf Ellaby	St Helens	1926–27
54	Johnny Ring	Wigan	1924–25
54	Brian Bevan	Warrington	1958–59

Goals in a Season

221	David Watkins	Salford	1972–73
219	Bernard Ganley	Oldham	1957–58
214	Kel Coslett	St Helens	1971–72
194	Lewis Jones	Leeds	1956–57
193	Jim Sullivan	Wigan	1933–34
193	Kel Coslett	St Helens	1970–71

193	David Watkins	Salford	1971–72
190	Bernard Ganley	Oldham	1958–59
189	Bernard Ganley	Oldham	1956–57
183	Fred Griffiths	Wigan	1961–62
183	Neil Fox	Wakefield	1961–62
183	David Watkins	Salford	1973–74
181	Billy Langton	Hunslet	1958–59
178	Jimmy Ledgard	Leigh	1954–55
178	Austin Rhodes	St Helens	1959–60
178	Geoff Pimblett	St Helens	1977–78
176	Bernard Ganley	Oldham	1959–60
175	David Watkins	Salford	1975–76
173	Eddie Tees	Bradford	1971–72
172	Sammy Lloyd	Hull	1978–79

Points in a Season

496	Lewis Jones	Leeds	1956–57
493	David Watkins	Salford	1972–73
476	David Watkins	Salford	1971–72
456	Neil Fox	Wakefield	1961–62
453	Bernard Ganley	Oldham	1957–58
453	Neil Fox	Wakefield	1959–60
452	Kel Coslett	St Helens	1971–72
438	David Watkins	Salford	1973–74
416	Austin Rhodes	St Helens	1959–60
404	Jim Sullivan	Wigan	1933–34
395	Kel Coslett	St Helens	1970–71
385	Colin Tyrer	Wigan	1969–70
385	David Watkins	Salford	1975–76
381	Geoff Pimblett	St Helens	1977–78
379	Nigel Stephenson	Dewsbury	1972–73
375	Steve Quinn	Featherstone	1979–80
373	Sammy Lloyd	Hull	1978–79
366	Steve Hubbard	Hull KR	1979–80
364	Eddie Tees	Bradford	1971–72
358	David Watkins	Salford	1970–71

Career Totals

Tries

800	Brian Bevan	Warrington and Blackpool	1946–64
477	Billy Boston	Wigan	1953–68
392	Albert Rosenfeld	Huddersfield, Wakefield and Bradford	1909–24
313	Joe Leytham	Lancaster and Wigan	1901–12
312	Jimmy Lomas	Bramley, Salford, Oldham and York	1900–23
303	Alan Hardisty	Castleford and Leeds	1958–74

Goals

2,859	Jim Sullivan	Wigan, Dewsbury, Keighley and Bradford	1921–46
1,768	Cyril Kellett	Hull KR and Featherstone	1956–74
1,322	David Watkins	Salford and Swinton	1967–80

1,171	Terry Clawson	Featherstone, Bradford, Hull KR, Leeds, Oldham, York, Wakefield, Huddersfield and Hull	1957–80
1,073	Kenny Gowers	Swinton	1954–73
1,030	Ronald James	Halifax	1961–71

Points

6,220	Neil Fox	Wakefield, Bradford, Hull KR and Bramley	1956–79
6,006	Jim Sullivan	Wigan, Dewsbury, Keighley and Bradford	1921–46
3,686	Cyril Kellett	Hull KR and Featherstone	1956–74
3,114	David Watkins	Salford and Swinton	1967–80
2,561	Terry Clawson	Featherstone, Bradford, Hull KR, Leeds, Oldham, York, Wakefield, Huddersfield and Hull	1957–80
2,340	Jimmy Lomas	Bramley, Salford, Oldham and York	1900–23

Australia

First Grade Premiership, Sydney:

	Winners	*Runners-up*
1908	South Sydney	Eastern Suburbs
1909	South Sydney	Balmain
1910	Newtown	South Sydney
1911	Eastern Suburbs	Glebe
1912	Eastern Suburbs	Glebe
1913	Eastern Suburbs	Newtown
1914	South Sydney	Newtown
1915	Balmain	Glebe
1916	Balmain	South Sydney
1917	Balmain	South Sydney
1918	South Sydney	Western Suburbs
1919	Balmain	Eastern Suburbs
1920	Balmain	South Sydney
1921	North Sydney	Eastern Suburbs
1922	North Sydney	Glebe
1923	Eastern Suburbs	South Sydney
1924	Balmain	South Sydney
1925	South Sydney	Western Suburbs
1926	South Sydney	University
1927	South Sydney	St George
1928	South Sydney	Eastern Suburbs
1929	South Sydney	Newtown
1930	Western Suburbs	St George
1931	South Sydney	Eastern Suburbs
1932	South Sydney	Western Suburbs
1933	Newtown	St George
1934	Western Suburbs	Eastern Suburbs
1935	Eastern Suburbs	South Sydney
1936	Eastern Suburbs	Balmain

1937	Eastern Suburbs	South Sydney/St George
1938	Canterbury-Bankstown	Eastern Suburbs
1939	Balmain	South Sydney
1940	Eastern Suburbs	Canterbury-Bankstown
1941	St George	Eastern Suburbs
1942	Canterbury-Bankstown	St George
1943	Newtown	North Sydney
1944	Balmain	Newtown
1945	Eastern Suburbs	Balmain
1946	Balmain	St George
1947	Balmain	Canterbury-Bankstown
1948	Western Suburbs	Balmain
1949	St George	South Sydney
1950	South Sydney	Western Suburbs
1951	South Sydney	Manly-Warringah
1952	Western Suburbs	South Sydney
1953	South Sydney	St George
1954	South Sydney	Newtown
1955	South Sydney	Newtown
1956	St George	Balmain
1957	St George	Manly-Warringah
1958	St George	Western Suburbs
1959	St George	Manly-Warringah
1960	St George	Eastern Suburbs
1961	St George	Western Suburbs
1962	St George	Western Suburbs
1963	St George	Western Suburbs
1964	St George	Balmain
1965	St George	South Sydney
1966	St George	Balmain
1967	South Sydney	Canterbury-Bankstown
1968	South Sydney	Manly-Warringah
1969	Balmain	South Sydney
1970	South Sydney	Manly-Warringah
1971	South Sydney	St George
1972	Manly-Warringah	Eastern Suburbs
1973	Manly-Warringah	Cronulla-Sutherland
1974	Eastern Suburbs	Canterbury-Bankstown
1975	Eastern Suburbs	St George
1976	Manly-Warringah	Parramatta
1977	St George	Parramatta
1978	Manly-Warringah	Cronulla-Sutherland
1979	St George	Canterbury-Bankstown
1980	Canterbury-Bankstown	Eastern Suburbs

Index